Research Methods for Language Teaching

Research Methods for Language Teaching

Inquiry, Process and Synthesis

Netta Avineri

Middlebury Institute of International Studies at Monterey, CA, USA

Applied Linguistics for the Language Classroom

Series Editor: Andy Curtis

First published 2017 by
PALGRAVE

Palgrave in the UK is an imprint of Macmillan Publishers Limited,
registered in England, company number 785998, of 4 Crinan Street,
London, N1 9XW.

Palgrave® and Macmillan® are registered trademarks in the United States,
the United Kingdom, Europe and other countries.

ISBN 978–1–137–56342–2 paperback

This book is printed on paper suitable for recycling and made from fully
managed and sustained forest sources. Logging, pulping and manufacturing
processes are expected to conform to the environmental regulations of the
country of origin.

A catalogue record for this book is available from the British Library.

A catalog record for this book is available from the Library of Congress.

Printed in China

Contents

Section IV: Bringing It All Together

List of Figures and Tables

Figures

Tables

Series Editor's Introduction

The purpose of this Applied Linguistics for the Language Classroom (ALLC) series is to help bridge what still appears to be a significant gap between the field of applied linguistics and the day-to-day classroom realities of many language teachers and learners. For example, Selivan recently wrote that "Much applied linguistics research remains unapplied, is often misapplied, or is downright inapplicable" (2016, p. 25). This gap appears to have existed for some time and has yet to be bridged. For example, in 1954, Pulgram published *Applied Linguistics in Language Teaching*, which was followed a few years later by Robert Lado's classic work, *Linguistics Across Cultures: Applied Linguistics for Language Teachers* (1957). However, we are still seeing articles 60 years later helping language teachers to apply linguistic theory to language lessons (Magrath, 2016).

Therefore, one of the features of this ALLC series that makes it distinctive is our focus on helping to bridge the ongoing gap between applied linguistics and language classrooms. Our envisaged readership for these books is busy classroom language teachers, including those entering the profession and those who have been in it for some time already. We also gave a lot of thought to what teachers completing a first degree in education, teachers doing MA-TESOL courses and language teachers completing other professional qualifications would find most useful and helpful.

Bearing such readers in mind, one of the ambitious goals of this ALLC series is to present language teachers with clear, concise and up-to-date overviews and summaries of what they need to know in key areas: Assessment; Methods and Methodologies; Technology; Research Methods; and Phonetics, Phonology and Pronunciation. Attempting to do what much larger and weightier volumes have attempted, but doing so in volumes that are slimmer and more accessible, has been a challenge, but we believe these books make an original and creative contribution to the literature for language teachers.

Another distinctive feature of this ALLC series has been our International Advisory Board, made up of Professor Kathleen M. Bailey and Professor David Nunan. These two outstanding figures in our field helped us to keep our target readers in mind and to stay focused on the classroom, while keeping the connections to applied linguistics, so we can advance the building of the bridges between applied linguistics and language classrooms.

In *Research Methods for Language Teaching: Inquiry, Process and Synthesis*, Netta Avineri covers a great deal of ground in relatively little space, making this an ideal book for language teachers who may be relatively new to research or who would like to expand their current knowledge of research methods in language education. Drawing on Wolcott's (1992) notion of "idea-driven research", Avineri's starting point is that "All research comes from a place of inquiry, ongoing questioning to better understand a phenomenon of interest in the world" (p. 9). Based on that starting point, she created the acronym ACE, in which A is for "applicable", C is for "collaborative", and E is for "empowering". Avineri also presents language teachers with a "methodological toolkit" to help them engage in the process of enquiry and strategies to help them develop what she refers to as a "research disposition", which she describes as "an approach to professional practice that involves continuous inquiry, responsiveness and change" (p. 10).

Setting research methods in the much broader context of how we live our lives, Avineri challenges the readers to contemplate fundamental questions, such as "do I believe that there are multiple truths or that there is only one?" and "Do I believe that individuals construct their realities or that there is a unified reality independent of our perceptions of it?" (p. 13).

These are not easy questions to answer, but they are effective ways of connecting our personal and professional lives so that they can feed into and come out of each other in mutually beneficial ways.

Readers are asked to consider other big questions: What is Culture? (Chapter 7), in relation to ethnographic approaches to research on language teaching and learning and in terms of classrooms as cultures, in which "Students and teachers constantly engage in language socialization practices ... [and] negotiate norms and beliefs as they relate to classroom interactions" (p. 121). Avineri also helps readers make important distinctions, for example between description, analysis and interpretation (Chapter 10), the differences between which are not always clear, when working with qualitative data.

A good example of an important recurring theme in this book is the notion of the "positionality" of the reader as a researcher, which is introduced in Chapter 3, in a discussion of naturalistic enquiry. In Chapter 7, in relation to ethnographic research, Avineri explains that "positionality" means recognizing "how your own perspectives and identities may have an impact on your findings and conclusions" and she emphasizes the importance of acknowledging "our own subjectivities" (p. 126), as we take on multiple roles during the research process. And at the end of the book, as an appendix, Avineri gives her own example of a positionality statement: "In order to situate this research more fully, it is essential that I reflect upon my own positionality within the contexts that are the focus of this research. I have thought in detail about the ways that my own history, choices and experiences have shaped my interest in and approach to this topic" (p. 202). (The importance of acknowledging our positionality is also discussed in Chapter 10.)

In total, the 12 chapters contain more than 60 Activities and Reflections that help readers apply the theory to the practice. There is also a comprehensive Glossary and around 30 Recommend Readings, which are accompanied by brief notes, and most of which have links to the readings as well as links to many more online resources. All of these features make this book a very useful introduction to what is available to help language teachers develop their research knowledge, skills and understanding.

Andy Curtis

Acknowledgements

I would like to thank my colleagues, students, family, and friends near and far who have provided me with encouragement throughout the process of writing this book. I greatly appreciate Palgrave Commissioning Editor Paul Stevens' and ALLC Series Editor Andy Curtis' ongoing guidance, which helped me to formulate my unique contributions to the ALLC series. Thank you to the Palgrave editorial staff, Cathy Scott and Robin Moul, for their expertise in facilitating this entire process. Kathi Bailey has consistently been a respected mentor, both in publishing and in language teacher inquiry. David Nunan's comprehensive and valuable input on all aspects of the book helped to shape my approach to writing a research methods book for a language teaching audience. Eduardo has been there all along the way, with constant words of motivation and inspiration. Eema has always been my advocate, in writing and in life. I have appreciated the distinctive perspectives of teacher-researchers, especially Tamar and Aaron. Thank you to my students; our interactions have informed my philosophies around language, language teaching, and research methods. A special note of gratitude goes to my MIIS students – they have been generous partners throughout this process of inquiry, allowing me to try out with them many concepts, activities, and resources that have now found a home in this book. All this support has been truly invaluable.

Introduction

When I began as an applied linguistics/TESL (teaching English as a second language) master's student at the University of California, Los Angeles, I remember looking forward to the opportunity to teach my first English as a second language (ESL) class with international, university-level students. I had tutored and taught language classes to students of various ages before then, in the United States and France. But I never felt truly equipped in terms of methods and approaches until I began my MA programme. One of the main reasons why I selected the UCLA programme was that it allowed me to learn about theory, research and practice while simultaneously giving me the opportunity to teach under the supervision of language teachers and mentors who had years of experience.

The first ESL class I taught was a four skills course for international students in a six-week summer programme, and I distinctly recall those first days of teaching because of all the questions I had. I always wanted to know more about what the research and theory said about what pedagogical approaches I should take, how second language acquisition works and how to better understand my students' linguistic and cultural backgrounds. I have continued to ask a range of research questions about the relationships among language education theory, research and practice ever since.

Since that time, I have taught language classes to students from all over the world, from oral skills courses for international teaching assistants to writing courses for students preparing for their master's in business administration to film-based language courses for students interested in the relationships between media and culture. I have since earned my doctorate and have begun my professional career as an applied linguist and linguistic anthropologist, researching diverse issues, including heritage language socialization, interculturality in language teacher education, language and social justice and service-learning. I have consistently found that in-depth inquiry has been an integral and essential aspect of my work. Becoming an action teacher-researcher has empowered me to ask critical questions about my own teaching and to think deeply about various way to improve my own practice. This has also allowed me to become part of a range of communities of practice also interested in the intersections between pedagogy and inquiry. This book is an outgrowth of my strong belief in an inquiry-based approach to teaching language. I now teach Linguistics and Education courses at the Middlebury Institute of International Studies at Monterey in the Teaching English to Speakers of Other Languages (TESOL) and Teaching Foreign Language (TFL) programmes, along with International Education Management and Intercultural Communication courses. In all of these courses I encourage my students to explore the various intersections among research and practice as they develop their own language teaching and programme administration philosophies and approaches.

Using my own experiences as a guide, this book is therefore designed to provide you with a range of approaches and tools for thinking deeply about conducting research in classrooms in which you teach, student teach, observe and develop curricula. My hope is that the book's style and content will encourage you to become part of a **community of practice** focused on inquiry, equipping you with relevant terminology and options for your own teaching and research. Throughout the book, I share with you various options and examples, along with pros and cons and rationales for each. This means that you can select which research approaches resonate with you and seem relevant to your own teaching. This is designed to empower you to engage in research, therefore democratizing who 'counts' as a researcher. The book highlights the various ways that research is engagement in humble inquiry. At its core research is a way of saying that we don't know yet – which then involves a disposition of humility to explore and discover what is happening in the world around us. The book also includes a range of activities and reflections that can be adapted for both pre- and in-service language teachers.

The types of questions that language teachers inquire about are frequently focused on four main areas: classroom management issues, methodological concerns, linguistic matters and sociolinguistic topics. Some example teacher questions might be the following:

- *Classroom Management Issues:* How often should I put students in groups? Is pair work always the best option? Is it okay if some students aren't talking? How do I teach to students who are more visual or auditory learners? How can I maximize my students' experience in my online language classroom?
- *Methodological Concerns:* Shall I use **inductive** or **deductive** approaches? How/when should I correct my beginning-level students – should I focus on fluency or accuracy to prevent **fossilization**? Is 'repeat after me' effective? Should I slow down my speech?
- *Linguistic Matters:* When should I teach which tenses? How helpful is it when I give my students lists of vocabulary words? How do I examine students' perceptions of their language ability and compare that with my own assessments of their language ability? How can I teach writing through reading (integrate modalities)?
- *Sociolinguistic Topics:* Which language variety should I use in class? How do I acknowledge and value students' home languages while teaching them a common second language (2)?

By including in each chapter key questions like these, the book will give you the chance to see yourselves and your inquiry as the starting point. This book will allow practitioner-researchers to move throughout the process of inquiry, including topics, literature reviews, research questions, research design, data collection/analysis, **arguments** and finally **pedagogical implications**. The collaborative nature of research is central to the book's approach.

This book has a number of unique features. First of all, it is designed to motivate you to become part of a practitioner-researcher community of practice. It does so by first taking the perspective of you as the teacher, as opposed to the distant researcher writing to the practising teacher. Second, it highlights that inquiry is the primary focus and that research methods should follow logically from that focus. For example, research questions may need multiple methods to be answered. Therefore, methods are not discussed in isolation but in relation to one another. Third, it emphasizes technologies and multiple modalities, both in terms of the current state of language learning environments and also in terms of research methods meant to capture these new complexities. Fourth, there are Reflections and Activities included throughout the book, for different levels and contexts. These are designed to speak to student teachers teaching in diverse classrooms and also to practising teachers interested in their own teaching environments. Fifth, the book will provide hands-on approaches to realistically conducting research while teaching, considering issues like time management and process. The book also includes details of online spaces where teachers can share with and mentor one another, and it provides tools for creating face-to-face research groups. A means for professional development, both for pre-service teachers newer to the field and in-service teachers currently seeking to broaden their theoretical and pedagogical repertoire, this book can help you to create meaningful, ongoing research links to your language-teaching practice. This book and its associated activities are designed to develop your identities as reflective practitioner-researchers (Schön, 1984) and allow you the opportunity to become part of a growing community of practice. The book is meant to serve as a resource, which can be used by both pre-service and in-service teachers for various languages in a range of contexts (K–12, adult school, community college and higher education institutions).

I have organized the book to take you through the various phases of inquiry, process and synthesis. Section I (Inquiry) focuses on foundational research concepts, literature review, research questions, research design and research ethics. Section II (Data Collection) includes information about naturalistic and psychometric approaches to the collection of **qualitative** and **quantitative** data. These include questionnaires, interviews, **focus groups**, reflections, case studies, ethnography, visual data, transcription and quantitative data. Section III (Data Analysis) provides guidance on both interpretive and statistical approaches to data analysis. Section IV (Bringing It All Together) includes approaches to building an argument, considering implications and becoming integrated into relevant communities of practice.

You are encouraged to use the book on your own, though it may be best if you are guided by a professor and/or use the book collaboratively with colleagues. You can also 'curate' the book based on your own interests, expertise and skill sets, selecting which aspects of the book are most useful for you. The book is not static – it is meant to be interactive as well as adaptable for various purposes. And a number of resources for further depth and exploration have been provided for you. I wish you all the best as you begin or continue on the road to inquiry. Good luck!

Suggested Reading

http://www.culi.chula.ac.th/Research/e-Journal/bod/David%20 Nunan.pdf
This resource provides a useful framework for considering how language teachers can be empowered to engage in their own classroom research.

Section I: Inquiry

How to ACE the Research Process

Guiding Questions:

1. What is research?
2. Have you conducted research before?
3. What are some topics you want to explore in your own classroom or future classrooms?
4. What are the main steps in the research process?

All research comes from a place of inquiry, ongoing questioning to better understand a phenomenon of interest in the world. This notion is described by Wolcott (1992) as 'idea-driven research' (p. 7). Research by and for language teachers can be applicable, collaborative and empowering: ACE. If you choose to do research in your language classroom, it is frequently because you are interested in finding out more about how to do your work more effectively. By engaging wholeheartedly in the process of inquiry (Graziano and Raulin, 2012), you can then *apply* your research findings to fostering a classroom environment that matches your language-teaching philosophy. The research process can also be *collaborative*. At the very least you are collaborating with members of your community of practice through reading and citing relevant literature, and at most you can discuss and work with other practitioners on research that is based on your interests. This means that you are never truly on your own when engaging in teacher research. The research process can be *empowering* in that you are able to capitalize upon your curiosity in order to contribute to your immediate environment, as well as to the field of language education more broadly. As teachers, you are knowledge producers in the realm of language education research. In this book, my goal is to provide you with a range of approaches that can facilitate your development of the knowledge, skills and attitudes associated with *applicable*, *collaborative* and *empowering* language education research. The book highlights strategies for developing a **research disposition**, an approach to professional practice that involves continuous inquiry, responsiveness and change.

This book will focus on inquiry, the ongoing critical questioning of a phenomenon of interest; the research process, the 11 steps of which are included below; and synthesis, the bringing together of multiple threads of argument. We will discuss research-shaped practice, informed by existing literature and also by research conducted by teachers themselves. This book provides language teachers with the **methodological toolkit** to engage in the process of inquiry (Graziano and Raulin, 2012) involved in conducting language classroom research (cf. Burnaford, Fischer, and Hobson, 2001; Fichtman Dana and Yendol-Hoppey, 2014; Higgins, Parsons, and Bonne, 2011). The book will take as its starting point those questions that you as language teachers inquire about in your daily practice and will then provide the tools for selecting the research methods that are appropriate to answer those questions.

Second Language Classroom Research

Second language classroom research is a growing field in applied linguistics (cf. Allwright and Bailey, 1991; Bailey and Nunan, 1996; Chaudron, 1988; Nunan and Bailey, 2009; Seliger and Long, 1983; Tarone, Gass and Cohen, 1994). It is important for all language teachers to learn from existing research so that it may inform their practice and also to engage in research themselves in order to contribute to their own and broader bodies of knowledge on central topics in the field (cf. McDonough and McDonough, 2014). The similarities and differences among classroom, teacher and action research (Bailey, 2014; Nunan and Bailey, 2009) are essential for teachers to grasp as a framework for situating their own research inquiry. Classroom research is conducted in classrooms and teacher research is conducted by teachers (on/in different contexts) (Nunan and Bailey, 2009). Action research is 'a form of research designed for practitioners that allows teachers, for example, to research practices, schools, students, communities, curriculum, and so on, for the purpose of improving their professional work' (Kincheloe, 2008, p. 20). In addition, Schachter and Gass (1994) highlight some of the central issues involved in conducting classroom research, which teachers should be aware of, including collaboration, combining pedagogical soundness and experimentally acceptable **practices**, political and social decisions that may interrupt the research, and sharing the results.

A merging of teacher and researcher expertise, skills and interests shape much of this book's focus. As Seliger and Long (1983) note, 'Good language teachers have always acted like researchers, realizing that language teaching and learning are very complex activities which require constant questioning and the analysis of problematic solutions' (p. v). They also highlight the fact that 'the language teacher and the researcher share the same goal: understanding what is involved in the process of second language acquisition' (ibid., p. vi).

This book will provide you with approaches to conducting research focused on both **ideologies** (belief systems) and practices (daily behaviours). It provides language teachers with a range of tools to investigate both what individuals and communities *believe* and what they *do* in diverse contexts. Taking an ecological approach (cf. van Lier, 2004) to language teaching, this book acknowledges the broader systems of which language classrooms are a part. For example, as opposed to focusing on one classroom and its students, some chapters will present tools for collecting data from other teachers, administrators and stakeholders within larger school systems. You can also use the book's material to focus on data using traditional language modalities, as well as digital literacy, texting, blogging and other multimodal literacies (cf. Vaish and Towndrow, 2010) in language classrooms and blended learning environments (cf. Tomlinson and Whittaker, 2013; Nunan and Bailey, 2009, pp. 20–21). This broadening of what counts as language learning research, beyond a focus on 'classrooms' (cf. Benson & Reinders, 2011), can allow language teachers in diverse contexts to adapt the materials for their own purposes.

The Research Process

The book is organized into four sections: Inquiry, Data Collection, Data Analysis and Bringing It All Together. Each section will provide you with reflections and activities to complete while you learn about the 11 steps in the research process (Fig. 1.1). Please note that these steps do not have to be followed in the order implied by the sequencing. Also, especially in naturalistic research, many of these steps are recursive. For example, you may begin collecting data and then realize you need to read up on a particular topic before engaging in analysis.

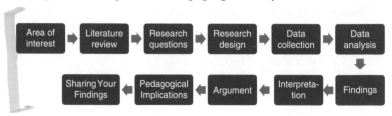

Figure 1.1 The Research Process

1. Establishing an area of interest ('topic': e.g. focus on form, interaction in asynchronous online environments)
2. Conducting a literature review (methods, gap, state of field): peer-reviewed articles and books, blogs, documentaries, reports, other institutions' reports and materials, personal communication
3. Developing research questions (inductive/deductive)
4. Selecting an appropriate research design (methods; e.g. questionnaires, interviews, focus groups, observations)

5. Data collection (e.g. piloting, sample selection)
6. Data analysis (interpretive, statistical)
7. Identification of findings
8. Interpretation of the analysis
9. Building an argument ('intended to persuade') (findings, compare to other literature)
10. Identification of implications (now what?)
11. Sharing of findings (e.g. articles, conferences, social media, reports)

The book focuses on creating a clear process and rationale for the design and the carrying out of **empirical** (data-based) research. Different chapters focus on the creation of research questions, inductive and deductive research, quantitative and qualitative data and data collection and analysis.

World Views Underpinning Research Methodological Choices

Every methodological choice in research is shaped by our views of the world. For example, do I believe that there are multiple truths, or that there is only one? Do I believe that individuals construct their realities, or that there is a unified reality independent of our perceptions of it? Mills and Birks (2014, p. 20, Table 2.1) provide a useful overview of research paradigms and their associated characteristics. They note that *positivism* "asserts the existence of a single reality that is there to be discovered" (p. 20). *Postpositivism* 'rejects the concept of a measurable reality that exists in isolation of the observer' (p. 20). *Postmodernism* 'posits that the reality of a phenomenon is subjectively relative to those who experience it' (p. 20). *Critical theory* 'seeks to redress societal injustices through research' (p. 20). *Constructivism* 'recognizes that reality is constructed by those who experience it and that research is a process of reconstructing that reality (p. 20).

Creswell (2014, p. 5) also discusses the interconnectedness of philosophical world views with research design and methods. He notes that a 'transformative worldview' holds that research inquiry needs to be intertwined with politics and a political change agenda to confront social oppression at whatever level it occurs (Mertens, 2010)' (Creswell, 2014, p. 9), which is similar to critical theory in Mills and Birks' typology. He also adds *pragmatism*, which is focused on 'actions, situations, and consequences. ... [T]here is a concern with applications – what works – and solutions to problems (Patton, 1990)' (Creswell, 2014, p. 10). As you consider how you might approach your own research, it is important to continuously question how your methodological choices may be shaped by your own world views.

REFLECTION 1.1

Which of the 5 world views listed above do you adhere to most closely? Why do you think that is? What experiences and interactions have helped to shape your world views? In what ways, if any, do you think these world views might have an impact on your research? Share your thoughts with a colleague if possible.

Diverse Research Approaches

A methodology is 'a particular social scientific discourse (a way of acting, thinking, and speaking) that occupies a middle ground between a discussion of methods (procedures, techniques) and discussions of issues in the philosophy of science' (Schwandt, 2007, p. 193). See Brown 2004, p. 496, Figure 19.6, for standards of research soundness continua for primary research and Creswell 2014, p. 18, Table 1.4, for qualitative, quantitative and mixed methods approaches.

Nunan and Bailey (2009) discuss two main research traditions: psychometric, in which 'the aim is to test the influence of different variables on one another' (p. 6), and naturalistic, in which 'the aim is to obtain insights into the complexities of teaching and learning through uncontrolled observation and description' (p. 7). They further highlight Grotjahn's (1987) discussion of the three aspects of research (p. 11): the design (experimental, quasi-experimental and nonexperimental), the data collected (quantitative or qualitative) and the type of analysis (statistical or interpretive). Though there are two 'pure' forms (psychometric – experimental design, quantitative data, statistical analysis – and naturalistic – nonexperimental design, qualitative data, interpretive analysis), a researcher could combine aspects of their framework to 'yield six mixed or "hybrid" forms' (p. 11). Generally speaking, the naturalistic paradigm is based on a constructivist world view, whereas the psychometric paradigm is based on a positivist or postpositivist paradigm.

Approaches to qualitative data collection include narrative research, phenomenology, grounded theory, ethnography and case studies and approaches to quantitative data collection include experimental and nonexperimental (Creswell, 2014, p. 12). Mixed methods may be convergent, explanatory sequential, or exploratory sequential (Creswell, 2014, p. 12). One might collect qualitative data through interviews, focus groups and reflections, with quantitative data being based on measures of test scores and Likert scale responses. Brown (2004, p. 490, Figure 19.5) provides a useful summary of the primary research characteristics, which has more complexity than the Grotjahn (1987) paradigm. Though in general the book will employ Grotjahn's (1987) paradigm, at times the Brown (2004) typology may be useful for you as well if further details or complexity are needed.

Brown notes that there are three main types of primary research: interpretive research (case studies, introspection, discourse analysis, interactional analysis, and classroom observation), survey research (interviews, questionnaires), and statistical research (descriptive, exploratory, quasi-experimental, experimental). He also highlights a quantitative–qualitative continuum spanning from qualitative–exploratory to quantitative–statistical. Below is a list of twelve features of these various research approaches (Brown, 2004, p. 490):

1. Data Type (Qualitative – Quantitative)
2. Data Collection Methods (Non-Experimental – Experimental)
3. Data Analysis Methods (Interpretive – Statistical)

4. Intrusiveness (Non-Intervention – High Intervention)
5. Selectivity (Non-Selective – Highly Selective)
6. Variable Description (Variable Definition – Variable Operationalization) *how you define variable*
7. Theory Generation (Hypothesis Forming – Hypothesis Testing)
8. Reasoning (Inductive – Deductive) *general → specific*
9. Context (Natural – Controlled)
10. Time Orientation (Longitudinal – Cross-Sectional)
11. Participants (Small Sample Size – Large Sample Size)
12. Perspective (Emic – Etic) ?

These features can provide a useful heuristic for determining the details of your research design as you plan out your own research projects.

REFLECTION 1.2

Based on your existing knowledge of research (from previous classes, research projects, literature reviews, etc.) which of the terms above are you familiar with? Which are you curious to know more about? Based on what you already know about research approaches where would your ideal research would fall along the continua listed above? Why? Share your thoughts with a colleague if possible.

A Note about Research Methods

Many discussions of research methods encompass false dichotomies (quantitative/qualitative (for more on this, see Brown 2004, p. 488), ideologies/practices, deductive/inductive). Though at first it may be useful to distinguish these various aspects of research, it may be even more helpful to think of these concepts as spectrums (see also Reichardt and Cook, 1979, p. 10, for a comparison of qualitative and quantitative research paradigms, reproduced in Brown, 2004, p. 487). For example, questionnaires can involve the collection of qualitative and quantitative data, as well as interpretive and statistical analysis. One can use interviews to talk about ideologies and also report on practices and decision making. Observation may help us understand ideologies, identities and practices. There are deductive–inductive hybrid research designs. And frequently, the strongest arguments involve synthesis, connections and triangulation among multiple research methods, all of which relate back to one's research question. One way to think through all of this complexity is to create a research proposal that helps solidify your plans and interests, which you can share with a colleague or mentor (cf. Paltridge and Phakiti, 2015, pp. 272–273). The process of receiving feedback on your proposal is a critical step in the research process and can help you to understand your research plan and details from another point of view. This can also facilitate your participation in a community of practice and will encourage you to provide feedback to others as well.

Time Management

Though conducting research can be quite rewarding, carving out time to engage in research can be difficult. Therefore, it is important to create timelines that acknowledge teachers' cyclical timing, break down the research process and select an appropriate scope for your research. For example, in terms of completing readings as you work on your literature review, I would recommend that you set a goal that is doable given the specific time constraints in your day/week. For example, if you teach Monday–Thursday at 9–3, you could plan to find 2–3 new sources every Friday 12–1. Here again, the goal is to create a research plan that is manageable, systematic and motivating.

The Writing Process

Throughout the research process, you will be writing at various phases and for different purposes (Wolcott, 2009). Creswell (2014) describes 'Writing as Thinking' and 'Habits of Writing' (pp. 84–86). For example, you might be taking brainstorming notes as you consider your possible topic(s) of interest. You could also draft multiple research questions to get feedback from a colleague or friend. The literature review process is also one of multiple drafts (discussed in more detail in Chapter 2). During the **coding** and memoing process, you create notes based on transcripts and textual material. I would encourage you to consider your preferences in terms of writing (place, amount of time, modality, etc.) and also identify particular people with whom you can engage in a fruitful feedback-and-revision process. See Creswell (2014) for detailed guidance on writing proposals, abstracts, introductions, literature reviews, research questions and purpose statements (along with examples for different research types).

Overview of the Book

Section I: Inquiry

This section outlines the process of research, beginning with topics of inquiry and moving to the literature review, research questions, data collection/analysis, findings, argument and finally pedagogical implications. It will highlight the ways that research methods are selected carefully in order to appropriately answer research questions and that methods can complement one another.

Chapter 1: How to ACE the Research Process

This chapter provides an overview of the research process and will highlight the importance of research-shaped practice, informed by existing literature and also by research conducted by teachers themselves. It also discusses approaches to argument and evidence, which be discussed in further detail in Section IV. The chapter provides an overview of inductive and deductive research, approaches to qualitative and quantitative data collection and **reliability** and **validity**.

Chapter 2: The Noun and the Verb of the Literature Review

This chapter focuses on various approaches to conducting and constructing a literature review, beginning with topics that one is interested in investigating. It includes a number of visual representations that can help teachers conceptualize which bodies of literature they are hoping to draw upon and contribute to. It will highlight a number of hands-on activities (e.g. annotated bibliographies, Venn diagrams, long/medium/close-up shots) as ways to think through the process of and build the product of the literature review. This chapter also emphasizes not only understanding literature but also critiquing it, in relation to one's chosen focus.

Chapter 3: Research Questions and Research Design: Concretizing Inquiry

This chapter discusses how to move from a topic to a research question that is answerable based on a particular research design. It discusses both inductive and deductive research questions. It also highlights how the literature review's purpose is to set up the research question as a means to fill an existing research gap. Finally, it includes a discussion of your creating implications questions, which your eventual argument may be able to inform.

Chapter 4: Research Ethics: Reasons, Roles, Responsibilities and Relationships

This chapter discusses ethical issues raised by research, including the management of roles (teacher vs researcher), **informed consent** and boundaries. In particular, it highlights how a teacher's identities and others' perceptions can shape the material one can reasonably attain. In addition, it emphasizes the **ethical dilemmas** involved in taking on a researcher role to analysing data that may have originally been shared for educational purposes when one was in a teacher role. It also provides strategies for approaching students and other stakeholders as a researcher and asking them to provide data (e.g. interviews).

Section II: Data Collection

This section highlights methods that capture and analyse ideologies, meaning individuals' and communities' perceptions, views and beliefs (in some literature called 'Introspective' data methods, cf. Nunan and Bailey, 2009) as well as those that capture and analyse practices, what individuals and communities do on a daily basis. The section focuses on how various methods of data collection can complement one another for the purpose of answering a particular research question (see Creswell, 2014, pp. 191–192 for options, advantages and limitations of various qualitative data collection types).

Chapter 5: Making Questionnaires Work for You

This chapter focuses on questionnaire design, including the range of question types and their positives and negatives, as well as the order of questions. It discusses if, how and when to effectively ask demographic questions. It provides tools for effective question design (cf. Boyd and Heritage, 2006; Clayman and Heritage, 2002), acknowledging that the ways that questions are constructed have a huge impact on the responses that will be provided. It discusses the possibilities of questionnaires (e.g. collecting a lot of data quickly) and their limitations (e.g. depending on what people say they believe or do). It also includes details about online tools (e.g. Google Docs, Survey-Monkey) for collecting survey data. In addition, it provides key questions to think about in relation to using questionnaire data in combination with other data collection methods like interviews and focus groups.

Chapter 6: Interviews, Focus Groups and Reflections

This chapter discusses the range of options for collecting interview data, on its own and in combination with other data collection methods. It provides an overview of open-ended, semi-structured and **structured interview** methods, as well as hands-on activities designed to allow you the opportunity to practise a variety of interview techniques. In addition to a treatment of focus groups as a potential methodology, it discusses the use of various types of reflection, using Murphy's (2014) discussion of reflection-in-action (present), reflection-on-action (past) and reflection-for-action (future) that builds upon Schön's (1984, 1987) research on reflective practitioners. The chapter highlights how you can create and analyse individual reflection journals and collaborative reflections to think through your own practice. It also provides tools and reflection prompts for your students, which can then be analysed using discourse analytic and content analytic methods. There will be some discussion of think-aloud and stimulated recall protocols, as modes of reflection.

Chapter 7: Case Studies, Ethnography and Visual Data

Chapter 7 focuses on case studies in applied linguistics as a key methodology for your research. In addition, it will focus on ethnography, 'the written description of the social organization, social activities, symbolic and material resources, and interpretive practices characteristic of a particular group of people' (Duranti, 1997, p. 85). In ethnography, the goal is an **emic** (insider's) view through long-term **participant-observation**. In this chapter, you have the opportunity to learn about ethnographic methods such as disciplined notetaking. This chapter also discusses various forms of visual data, including photographs, maps and continuous monitoring. There is also a discussion of issues related to video- and audio-recordings, including frame grabs and subtitles, for a range of research purposes.

Chapter 8: Transcription: Process and Product

This chapter will highlight the range of transcription conventions for a variety of purposes, as a step towards **discourse analysis** and **content analysis**. Discourse analysis for language teachers (cf. McCarthy, 1991) will be highlighted as a means to examine in-class interactions, technology-facilitated interactions (e.g. AdobeConnect) and real-life interactions that can be used to teach descriptive language norms to one's class. It will also be discussed as a tool that teachers can teach to students, to collect data on real-life language use and authentic materials as a means to grasp descriptive language norms. Classroom data in the form of transcripts are included in this section.

Chapter 9: Approaches to Collection of Quantitative Data

This chapter discusses approaches to collection of quantitative data for examining individual and community practices and ideologies (for further exploration, see Plonsky, 2015). We will discuss different quantitative research designs, **variables**, levels of measurement, reliability, validity, **replicability** and **sampling**. These will be discussed as they connect to deductive research questions.

Section III: Data Analysis

This section will provide an overview of approaches to the analysis of qualitative data and quantitative data.

Chapter 10: Interpretive Analysis of Qualitative Data

The interpretive analysis process will be discussed in relation to qualitative data. We will focus on selecting the appropriate data analysis method (e.g. coding, discourse analysis, content analysis) for identifying patterns and themes in the particular data you have collected. We will then discuss some steps for engaging in these different qualitative data analysis methods.

Chapter 11: Approaches to Analysis of Quantitative Data

This chapter will focus on core concepts in analysis of quantitative data. It will discuss frequency and percentage distributions, **descriptive statistics** and **inferential statistics** options.

Section IV: Bringing It All Together

This section will synthesize the material presented thus far, focusing on the ways that in-depth analysis of various forms of data can be brought together into our argument, a discourse intended to persuade that establishes a position through rational support (Belcher, 2012, pp. 82, 87). It will focus on the ways that teachers can move from evidence and argument to what this may mean for one's teaching. And lastly this section will discuss how practitioner-researchers can become part of a community of practice.

Chapter 12: Arguments, Implications and Communities of Practice

This chapter provides approaches to creating an argument based on convincing evidence, especially considering one's eventual goals and audience. It also relates back to the research questions, ensuring that the argument does in fact answer them. It will then move from evidence and argument to possible implications for one's teaching. In particular, readers will be exposed to sample lesson plans that demonstrate how research can inform teaching practice. It also provides approaches to sharing one's research with others, throughout the research process and afterwards. It is designed to help practitioner-researchers build a community of practice where mentoring of various types occurs and in which different types of knowledge and expertise are valued.

Conclusion

Your questions and areas of interest may originate from the literature and/or from your classroom. Engaging in inquiry can therefore be an **iterative process**, in which research and teaching are mutually constitutive. For example, you might create a lesson/curriculum/assessment and measure its effects, and then be responsive to the results you find in the ways you teach from that point on. Throughout the research process, you can ask yourself some questions: Who are the people I want to connect with and learn from? To whom is my research relevant? By engaging in ongoing inquiry you can then apply your findings to your own practice and to the field of language education more broadly. Good luck!

Suggested Readings

Paltridge, B. and Phakiti, A. (eds) (2015). *Research Methods in Applied Linguistics: A Practical Resource.* London, UK: Bloomsbury Publishing.

This book is an incredibly useful and comprehensive resource for research in applied linguistics. The first half of the book provides overviews of key research methods (e.g. case studies, survey research), and the second half shares practical insights for research in particular areas of applied linguistics (e.g. research speaking, researching motivation).

Denzin, N.K. and Lincoln, Y.S. (eds) (2003). *Collecting and Interpreting Qualitative Materials.* Thousand Oaks, CA: SAGE Publications.

This edited volume provides detailed information about various modes of qualitative data collection and interpretation, from scholars in a range of disciplines.

Richards, K. (2003). *Qualitative Inquiry in TESOL.* Basingstoke: Palgrave Macmillan.

This book provides a useful overview of naturalistic, qualitative and action research inquiry, especially for applied linguistics and language teaching.

http://www.sjsu.edu/faculty/masucci/InterpretingQualitative Data.pdf

This PowerPoint from a professor at San Jose State University includes clear explanations of qualitative data.

CHAPTER 2

The Noun and the Verb of the Literature Review

Guiding Questions:

1. When was the last time you read something related to your work?
2. What did you read?
3. Where did you find it?
4. Do you remember its main ideas? Why or why not?
5. Did you share what you read with someone else? If so, with whom, and how?

A Research Disposition

The previous chapter highlighted strategies for developing a 'research disposition', an approach to professional practice that involves ongoing inquiry, responsiveness and change. This research disposition facilitates your involvement in communities of practice (Eckert and McConnell-Ginet, 1992; Lave and Wenger, 1991; Wenger, 2000) relevant to your daily work and can involve you in the broader project of meaningful language education.

This chapter will provide a scaffolded approach to conducting and constructing a literature review, beginning with topics that you are interested in knowing more about, identifying guiding questions and then moving into the four essential steps: understanding, organizing, dialoguing/critiquing and synthesizing literature. These four steps are important as a goal on their own and can also provide an important stepping stone before you would conduct your own research. A number of visual representations and hands-on activities focused on process and product (e.g. annotated bibliographies, Venn diagrams, long/medium/close-up shots) will be provided, which can help you conceptualize which bodies of literature you are hoping to draw upon and contribute to. I will also discuss approaches to writing a literature review, for those who are interested in providing a synthetic product for a particular purpose.

Literature Review: Making it Work for You

This chapter, like any effective language classroom, is differentiated (cf. Tomlinson, 2014). You are encouraged to select the aspects of the chapter that are most useful for, relevant to and doable for you. You can pick and choose which aspects of the process and product are applicable given your goals and interests. A literature review can be a marathon or a sprint, depending upon your needs and the kinds of literature that is accessible to you. Remember, though, that even a marathon has an end point – it is not designed to go on forever. I highly recommend that you set manageable goals along the way. The main idea is that the literature review process integrates you into communities of practice that are relevant to your current and future goals.

What is Literature?

In this book, I will consider literature to be any written document or media source that provides you with information that can be applied to your professional practice. For example, perhaps at a recent faculty meeting, a fellow teacher shares a recent blog post that makes you think about how you could work with bilingual students in your classroom. That is 'literature'. A publication on dual language learners from the Center for Applied Linguistics in Washington, DC, that you file away for summer reading is 'literature'. And a more traditional definition of literature, which includes scholarly (ideally peer-reviewed) publications, counts as well. As you begin thinking about your own research, consider whether you would adhere to a **broad definition** of literature, which would include any of the sources in the list below, or a **narrow definition** of literature (sources written by academic scholars that would be found in online databases and university libraries).

Source Types for Literature

A. Listservs related to your field (e.g. http://iteslj.org/links/tesl/discussion/)
B. Blog posts written by current practitioners
C. Scholarly journals/online articles
D. Professional organization websites and publications
E. Academic books
F. Media websites with series that feature content about language and culture (e.g. TED Talk, NPR)
G. What other sources of literature have you found to be useful in your own professional philosophy and practice? Add them to this list.

The decision about how to approach the literature review is based on your own interests, goals and time.

ACTIVITY 2.1

Join a listserv that interests you (http://iteslj.org/). For one week, monitor the types of posts that are shared on this listserv. What do you notice about the posts? Do you believe that staying on this listserv will provide you with the information you are interested in? Why? Why not?

ACTIVITY 2.2

Discuss with a colleague which of the source types you know of would be most and least credible. Why? Create a list of five criteria to determine credibility in the literature review sources you draw upon.

REFLECTION 2.1

At this point, considering your professional and personal commitments, would you conduct a literature review as a goal on its own? (If so, would you use a broad or a narrow definition of 'literature'?) Or would you conduct a literature review as a means towards another end (i.e. conducting your own original research project)? What would facilitate the process of conducting your own research?

Literature Review: Noun and Verb

A literature review identifies what others have said or discovered about a particular topic and can set up a research question (in deductive research, known as a research hypothesis) (Dörnyei, 2007; Islam, 2008; Nunan, 1992, Rabbi and Kabir, 2014; Seliger and Shohamy, 1990). The literature review is frequently conceptualized as a *noun* – something that one needs to read or write. What is talked about less often is the literature review *verb* – the process involved in reviewing literature about a particular topic, identifying themes and carving out one's own research focus (cf. Machi and McEvoy, 2012). The 'verb' is a discovery process, which includes (1) Understanding, (2) Organizing, (3) Dialoguing/Critiquing, (4) Synthesizing, (5) Reporting and (6) Becoming. In some sense, this literature review typology mirrors many of the steps in

Bloom's Taxonomy, in order: remembering, understanding, applying, analysing, evaluating and creating (https://cft. vanderbilt.edu/guides-sub-pages/blooms-taxonomy/). Each of these steps is no small feat – they involve a balance of humility and confidence about one's own voice and the contributions you hope to make to your daily practice and to the field.

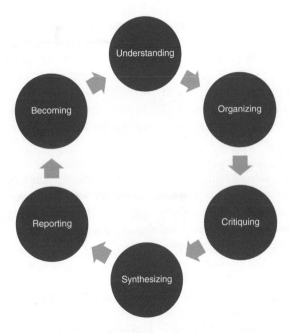

Figure 2.1   Literature Review Discovery Process

This chapter will first focus on the verb (the process), recognizing that it is made up of cyclical phases (Seliger and Shohamy, 1990). What is presented in this chapter is not designed as a perfectly chronological to-do list; the process is iterative, and you may go through each phase multiple times. I will then consider the noun (the product), with ways to conceptualize the organization of the literature review, in addition to some approaches to the language and organization of the literature review itself.

Selecting a Topic

Connected Noticing

The more time that one spends in language classrooms (as learners, observers, student teachers, or teachers) the more one notices particular patterns. This process can be considered 'open noticing', in which everything is potentially interesting. Frequently, however, you notice patterns in a classroom that connect with something you have seen in another classroom or with something you have read. This 'connected noticing', based upon patterns you observe over time, can be the beginning of effective research that is designed to answer particular questions; it helps to move you in the direction of selecting a focused topic, building a useful literature review and ultimately creating research question(s) for your own original research.

What is a Topic?

A 'topic' is something you are interested in knowing more about, and it should be specific enough so that you can go into depth while being broad enough that it could be interesting and relevant to teachers and researchers other than yourself.

For example, perhaps you are realizing that you are having a difficult time when your students are in groups, especially with jigsaw reading activities[1] because the students are at a range of language levels. You could start with the topic 'classroom management', but this would probably be too broad – it may be difficult to create a literature review that would be focused enough for your purposes (e.g. changing your professional practice, developing your own research questions). However, 'group work with multi-language-level classes' could

---

1 In jigsaw reading activities, you divide students into groups, each of which focuses on a particular section of one reading or on different readings. Students become "experts" on their section of reading and become like ambassadors of their focal material for other groups. Jigsaw reading activities serve many purposes, including reading comprehension, summary and synthesis and presentation skills.

be a specific enough topic, which would be a great starting point for a literature review. At this stage it is essential to figure out what other people have studied and learned about this topic, to help you decide what has already been discovered and shared about your chosen topic.

REFLECTION 2.2

Select a topic of interest in your context (e.g. practicum teaching site). Share your topic with a colleague (via email or in person) and have an inquiry-based discussion about it. What are two or three things you learned about the topic through discussion with your colleague? Can these two or three things help you during your literature review process? If so, how?

The Searching and Finding Process

Now that you have selected a topic, you can begin the process of searching for and finding sources that would be useful to you. Below are a few ways to approach this process. Professional organizations frequently have publications on their websites (free and accessible either to anyone or to those who are organizational members).

ACTIVITY 2.3

Go to a website for a professional organization that interests you (e.g. Center for Applied Linguistics in Washington, DC; TESOL in your state; TESOL; ACTFL). You can check out 'Professional Development Opportunities' at http://www.tc.columbia.edu/tesol/. Find at least one publication on the website that relates to your professional interests. Was it easy to find the publication? Why? Why not? Would you go back to this website for additional resources in the future? Why? Why not?

Useful Resources

The ERIC Thesaurus has education-related terms called descriptors that can provide you with starting places for your literature review. Studying these descriptors can be an effective way to ascertain key concepts and trends in your field of interest (Seliger and Shohamy, 1990). Another option is to start with existing reference lists (e.g. www.tirfonline.org), which are comprehensive collections of materials around particular topics. These can be a very useful 'one-stop shop' for relevant research and an easy way to get a sense of central themes in the field. Easily accessible literature reviews (an example is provided in the Online Resources part of this chapter) are another great starting point.

Google Scholar (scholar.google.com) is another 'one-stop shop' that can provide you with many of the 'narrow-definition' literature sources you may be looking for. In Google Scholar you can organize what you find into 'sort by relevance' or 'sort by date' depending on your needs. You can take a backward-looking approach by reading the references section of relevant research, to see lists of what they cited. You can also take a forward-looking approach by using Google Scholar's 'cited by' function to see which articles have cited the one you are reading. You may begin to see that certain journals publish the types of research you are interested in – some are more theory oriented, some more empirical (data) oriented and some more pedagogy oriented. If you are currently at an educational institution that has access to scholarly publications, you could then move from what you find in Google Scholar to accessing the journals and articles themselves. Databases in education and linguistics can also provide comprehensive lists of journals, articles and books relevant to your topic. Simply select the tools that are most easily accessible and useful for your particular context, goals and circumstances.

The Art of Search Terms

Once you have selected the tools that you will use to search for and find your sources, you will need to create search terms that will yield the most useful results in the most efficient way. Picking the perfect search terms is more an art than a science. Each search term will take you down a particular path (some say a 'rabbit hole') that may (or may not) ultimately provide the information you are seeking.

Below (Table 2.1) is an example of an ESL teacher's research topic, guiding question and search terms, which begin broad and become more and more specific. As you can see, the literature review process can uncover a variety of details related to your topic that you were not expecting but which can help you immensely in refining your focus and your interests. Based on the literature review discovery process, this teacher may realize that what he is actually interested in is whether spoken corrective feedback should be delayed or immediate, and whether he should be the one to provide it or if it would be more effective if peers shared feedback as well. This 'funnelling' of your search terms can guide the literature review process and the eventual creation of specific research questions (to be discussed in Chapter 3).

Table 2.1 Search Term 'Funnelling'

Context: Intermediate-level ESL classroom in a university setting
Example research topic: Error correction
Guiding question: Should I correct every spoken error or let my students express themselves?

Search terms:
"Error correction", "Corrective feedback"
"Corrective feedback ESL"
"Corrective feedback ESL university"
"Corrective feedback ESL university speaking"
"Corrective feedback ESL university speaking intermediate-level"

May find more specific information:
Recasts, writing feedback, learner uptake, delayed vs immediate, direct vs indirect, fluency vs accuracy, teacher vs peer vs self

This search process, no matter how it unfolds, is valuable – even if you do not immediately end up with what you believe would be most relevant to your interests. For example, let us say you are interested in creating a research project focused on inclusive teaching strategies for heritage learners in your classroom. You could start with 'heritage language' or 'heritage learners', but this will most likely give you theoretical and empirical research that may not be relevant to your pedagogical interests. Therefore, you could add the words 'strategies', but that might give you strategies that heritage learners themselves use in classrooms. Then you could add 'pedagogical' to see if you get what you're looking for. You may find a few relevant sources. However, in this case, what you may ultimately discover is that heritage languages is a new field and that there may not be as much research as you had hoped on exactly what you are interested in. But in the process, you may still find very useful, accessible online resources (e.g. www.nhlrc.ucla.edu, www.hlj.ucla.edu).

It may at first be frustrating to not find exactly what you were hoping for in a small amount of time. However, if you are designing your own research project, this process may in fact be instructive in that you can see how your original research could contribute to the field and also what might be complementary to and generalizable from what you are looking at. There is therefore an ongoing dialogue between your 'original' interests and your interests as they are being shaped and emerge, based on what you see already exists in the literature. In fact, judging how specific or general your search terms are can in fact help you track where you are in your overall literature review process. As this section has demonstrated, this beginning phase of the literature review is an opportunity to be exposed to new information in order to shape your interests and your original research in more specific ways.

REFLECTION 2.3

Reflect upon a language classroom you have learned in or taught in. What have you noticed in this setting that you might want to learn more about? Identify a specific topic and a guiding question. Using 'artful' search terms, find at least three online sources that would help you better understand what researchers have discovered about this topic. What are the titles of these sources?

The Reading Process

Once you have found sources that are relevant to your chosen focus, you can begin the reading process. As you read, you are attempting to understand a given field. The depth and breadth of the reading process will depend on the number of sources you have and on where you are in the reading process. For example, let us say that you have found ten sources that seem potentially relevant to your interests. You could select two or three that seem especially connected to your work and read those in great depth. You may take notes and highlight the sources as you are reading. There may be a few others that seem tangentially related to your interests, and you may read those more strategically (e.g. skimming and scanning) (cf. Ferris and Hedgcock, 2009).

All of these sources will also have a references section, which may create additional lists of readings that you would like to complete. Once you access those sources, you may find that you can read them more and more strategically, as through the reading process itself, your interests and your focus are becoming more crystallized. Strategic reading may involve grasping the main ideas through reading the abstract, identifying the argument in the introduction, reading the literature review sections in detail, skimming the methods section, finding two or three key ideas from the analysis section and checking your understanding by reading the conclusion. At different phases of the reading process, you may find different sections of the readings more or less relevant for your particular purposes (e.g. reading many methods sections in detail while you are constructing your own methods section). Eventually, you will be able to figure out very quickly whether or not the literature you are reading will be useful for your research interests.

REFLECTION 2.4

How do you prefer to read literature (online, printed out; in your office, at home)? When you find a source that interests you, what makes you keep reading?

ACTIVITY 2.4

Find a 'narrow-definition' literature source that is relevant to your interests. Read only the abstract, the introduction and the conclusion. What is the main idea of the reading? What additional information are you interested in finding out, based on what you know so far?

Organizing

Some language teachers, especially if they are new to this kind of reading, can begin to get overwhelmed as they read more and more sources. As mentioned in the previous section, every source you read has its own references section, and at first you may think that it is necessary to find and read all of the sources you come across. One way to handle this part of the reading process is to create *spreadsheets* that can organize the material and then be sorted for specific purposes (e.g. by author, year of publication, concepts).

As you read, you will begin to see patterns, in terms of concepts and trends in the field. This is when an **annotated bibliography** can come in handy. An annotated bibliography is a very useful tool in which you create a summary and an evaluation of each source you are reading, and it is a very effective way to get in the habit of understanding and synthesizing the literature you are reading. One tip to keep in mind is that annotated bibliographies should have no (or very few) direct quotes from the source itself. This pushes you to demonstrate your own account and assessment of the source as it relates to your interests. In many cases, the annotated bibliography can in fact become the first draft of your own written literature review product.

A second approach to organizing the literature review is to create a **Venn diagram**. Here, you identify three main concepts in the literature that you are drawing upon. For example, if you are reading literature before creating an action research project focused on balancing grammar teaching with student motivation in an online environment, then the literature you are drawing upon would fall into three broad categories – grammar instruction, motivation and online language teaching. Some of the literature you are reading will fit squarely into one of those categories, while others may lie at the intersection of multiple categories. The literature you find that would be at the intersection of all three categories would be the most relevant for your research. One way to approach the use of the Venn diagram is to number the sources in your annotated bibliography and then place those numbers in the different parts of the Venn diagram. You may then see which aspects of your literature review are more developed and what you still need to search for. In some cases, this part of the process may cause you to rethink the actual focus of your interests and your research. You can return to this exercise at various points in the process.

Once you have organized the literature in an intuitive way, then you can move to the dialoguing and critiquing stage of the process.

ACTIVITY 2.5

Think about a research project you would like to conduct in your own classroom. Which areas of literature would constitute the 3 circles in your Venn diagram? Why these circles? Are there any other areas that you think may be relevant at this point? Now try to find at least 1 source that fits into each of these 3 circles. Was this process easy or difficult for you? Why?

Dialoguing and Critiquing

After moving through the stages of choosing a topic, finding sources, reading sources and organizing those sources, you can begin to dialogue with and ultimately critique what you are reading. What does it mean to 'dialogue' with your sources? This involves your being part of a professional and scholarly conversation (Clark, 2005). Identifying three or four *text partners* (Clark, 2005, p. 147) can be a means of focusing research questions and entering the scholarly discussion. You can then imagine these personified texts involved in a conversation and imagine yourselves participating in that conversation, listening politely, connecting with points already made and identifying three or more points that would interest the chosen partners.

Critiquing is the process of asking critical questions about the literature you are reading, considering alternatives to what has been done, and imagining what would have made the

ACTIVITY 2.6

Author:

Title:

Reference:

The thesis/argument of this article is:

The most interesting ideas in this article are:

Why do I find these ideas interesting?

What aspects of the topic does this article overlook or distort?

If I were to write to the author of this article discussing these ideas, I might say the following:

A potential use of this article for my research is:

(from Clark 2005, Appendix 2)

research more effective. Among other benefits, this process helps determine how your own research can be most effective for your particular purposes. At first, critiquing what you read can be difficult, as it not simply about learning the language to critique and then sitting down to write a critique. When reading literature (especially a 'narrow-definition' literature source), I might at first think that if it was published it must be right. But, as I become more and more comfortable reading such literature, I realize that there are a number of areas I can ask critical questions about, in the interest of moving the field forward. Areas for critical questioning include study purpose, research questions, argument, study design and literature review (Harris, 2014).

ACTIVITY 2.7

Find a source and read its literature review. How is the literature review organized? Is it in dialogue with the sources? Does it critique the sources? What words are being used to present the sources?

ACTIVITY 2.8

Select a "narrow-definition" source and use the Harris (2014) areas listed above (study purpose, research questions, argument, study design, and literature review) to critique it.

Synthesizing

At this point you have begun to see links among different sources and can begin to synthesize the material you are reading. Once you move into this phase of writing a literature review, your ultimate goal is to move from an author-driven literature review to an idea-driven literature review. An author-driven literature review provides information about what specific sources say, with little connection among various sources, whereas an idea-driven literature review demonstrates connections within the literature and overall conversations and debates that various scholars are having with one another. An example of integrated literature review sentence would begin with the focal concepts and then provide the relevant citations: 'A commonly held belief in the field of second language education is that cooperative learning maximizes second language acquisition by providing opportunities for both language input and output (Fathman and Kessler, 1993; Holt, Chips, and Wallace, 1992; Long and Porter, 1985; McGroarty, 1993)' (Liang, Mohan, and Early, 1998). Many discrete literature reviews include a series of sentences that start with the author's name and then provide their ideas. Integrated literature reviews are more effective, as they emphasize *relationships* among ideas and overall trends within the field.

Writing the Literature Review

Throughout the literature review process you may be taking notes, creating annotations and jotting down ideas about the work that you are reading. All of these steps contribute to the overall writing process; therefore, there is not a discrete point at which you stop reading and start writing. However, there is a phase at which you begin to spend less time reading and more time writing. Here, you can keep in mind that you are not simply listing literature on a given topic but that your goal is to highlight 'criticality, relevance, and voice' (Rabbi and Kabir, 2014, p. 168). Depending on its purpose and venue, a literature review (and its sections) can vary in terms of length (Dörnyei, 2007), scope and sequence.

There are a number of major questions that a literature review can answer (Hart, 1998; Seliger and Shohamy, 1990). The literature review that you write does not need to address all of items in the list below. However, it would be a good idea to select at least two from this list that you would like to focus on (at least at first) (Hart, 1998):

A. key sources
B. major issues & debates
C. origins & definitions of the topic
D. key theories, concepts, & ideas
E. main questions & problems addressed to date
F. knowledge on how the topic is structured & organized

As discussed above, an annotated bibliography can provide a useful starting point for your written literature review. You could also create an outline (Criollo, 2003) that stems from your Venn diagram.

As you read other sources, it may be difficult to decide how to discuss those sources in your own literature review. At first you may use direct quotes, and eventually you can move to paraphrasing and summarizing, as these are focused accounts that connect to your research focus. The way you present each source will depend on its relevance, how it connects to your other sources and the overall argument that you seek to make with your literature review. One important point to keep in mind is that if you use a source that interprets a previous source, make sure to go back to the original source so that you can interpret it appropriately and connect it most closely to your research focus.

Organizing the Literature Review

When organizing the literature review, it is important to begin with the section that frames the other sections that are to come. In the example discussed above in relation to the Venn diagram, I identified three main categories: grammar instruction, motivation and online language teaching. If, for example, you begin your literature review with a section on grammar instruction and then move to motivation and then online language teaching, then your readers may think that what you are really interested in is grammar instruction, with the other two foci becoming secondary and tertiary. However, if you were to begin with a section on online language teaching, then you are communicating to your readers that that is your primary interest and the others are secondary and tertiary. In other words, the macro-level organization of literature reviews is an implicit expression of one's research priorities.

Another more micro-level organizational issue can arise when you are considering how much detail you would like to include about each source. This is where a film metaphor of long, medium and close-up shots (Rudestam and Newton, 2014), which refer to how distant or how close the camera is, can be useful. Similar to the Venn diagram, this tool can guide you in determining which sources you should discuss in great detail and which can have shorter treatment. Long shots are those sources that tend to be older and focused on a single concept/topic (perhaps one of your Venn diagram circles). Medium range are sources that move from older to newer, address more than one relevant topic and may have similar methodologies to your study. Close-ups are the latest research on your topic and have the highest intersection of methods and topics. For example, a source that is in the middle of your Venn diagram because it focuses on all three of your core concepts and also used the same methods you are considering is centrally relevant to your research. It would therefore be a 'close-up', and you would discuss it in great detail in your literature review. This detail would be expressed via direct quotes, paraphrasing and summarizing (https://owl.english.purdue.edu/owl/resource/563/01).

The language you use in the literature review also provides the reader with information about your stance towards particular sources and bodies of literature. You can achieve coherence through transition words and sentence connectors (Swales and Feak, 2012) and can integrate sources through particular verbs, phrases and expressions (Criollo, 2003).

ACTIVITY 2.9

Select three sources that are part of the same Venn diagram category. Practise presenting them in an integrated fashion, using specific language to achieve coherence and integrate sources. Did you find this easy or difficult? What strategies could you use to facilitate this process in the future?

ACTIVITY 2.10

Join a listserv that interests you (http://iteslj.org/links/TESL/ Discussion/). For one week, monitor the types of posts that are shared on this listserv. What do you notice about the posts? Do you believe that staying on this listserv will provide you with the information you are interested in? Why? Why not?

ACTIVITY 2.11

Select one of your 'text partners' and use the following guide to select an essential direct quote, an idea to paraphrase and a section to summarize. http://www.aquinas.edu/library/pdf/Para phrasingQuotingSummarizing.pdf

Did you find this exercise easy or difficult? What strategies can you identify for facilitating the process of deciding among quoting, paraphrasing and summarizing?

ACTIVITY 2.12

Read the following section of the literature review from Ushioda (2009, p. 217). What do you notice about how the section is organized, in addition to how it is in dialogue with and how it critiques previous literature? How does it set up an argument to come in their paper?

'With the transition from social psychological towards more cognitive perspectives in the 1990s, research on language motivation also sharpened its focus on contextual factors, partly in response to Crookes and Schmidt's (1991) call for more classroom-based concepts of motivation. Thus, Dörnyei (2005, pp. 74–83) has christened this phase the "cognitive-situated" period of language motivation research, with its sharper focus on features of the micro-context in which learning is situated, such as teaching methods or communicative styles and task design or participation structures.

Yet when we examine studies that take a more "situated" approach, we find that there is a tendency to rely on students' self-reported perceptions of their learning environment (e.g. student perceptions of teachers' communicative styles in Noels et al., 1999, or of instructional strategies in Jacques, 2001).'

Setting Up Your Research Questions

Ultimately, the goal of the literature review is to identify research gaps and therefore set up your original research questions. This means that your research is unique and novel. In some cases, you may also find a study that you wish to replicate, so that you can compare your findings to those in the published study. An effective literature review demonstrates what already exists and will then lead the reader to wonder why *your* research has not been done yet. Your research will focus on an issue that has not been sufficiently examined in the literature to date – focused on a new context, a specific group of learners, a different set of methodologies – something that makes your work a new contribution to what is already part of the literature. The next step then is to create research questions that are answerable with the data you plan to collect. Now that you know the existing literature, it is your turn to contribute to it.

Online Resources

Teachers College Columbia University TESOL Professional Development Opportunities:
http://www.tc.columbia.edu/tesol/index.asp?Id=Resources&Info=Professional+Development+Opportunities

ERIC Thesaurus Descriptors:
> http://library.albany.edu/subject/tutorials/education/eric_descriptors.html#teach

'Easily Accessible Literature Review':
> http://teslcanadajournal.ca/index.php/tesl/article/viewFile/698/529

Choosing the Right International Journal in TESOL and Applied Linguistics:
> https://www.academia.edu/2064493/Choosing_the_right_international_journal_in_tesol_and_applied_linguistics

Databases Example:
> http://www.miis.edu/academics/library/find/articles/education

Annotated Bibliography:
> http://guides.library.cornell.edu/annotatedbibliography

Critiquing a Source:
> http://www.usc.edu/hsc/ebnet/res/Guidelines.pdf

Writing a Literature Review:
> https://owl.english.purdue.edu/owl/resource/994/04/

Research Questions and Research Design: Concretizing Inquiry

3

Guiding Questions:

1. What is research?
2. What questions do you have about your students and your classroom?
3. What kinds of research can you reasonably undertake?
4. Is there research you have read that interests you?
5. Are there other educators with whom you have regular contact that you could talk about your research with?

Introduction

As discussed in Chapter 1, research is engagement in inquiry with the goal of understanding a phenomenon in the world through the systematic collection, analysis and interpretation of data. This chapter will discuss how to move from a topic you are interested in to a research question that is answerable based on a particular research design. It will discuss both inductive and deductive research questions. It will also highlight how the literature review's purpose is to set up the research question as a means to fill an existing research gap. It will also include a discussion of your creating a 'pedagogical implications' question, which your eventual argument may be able to be responsive to.

In the previous chapter, we discussed the process and product of a literature review, highlighting the ways that engaging with literature can help you to identify your specific research interests and the research gap you hope to fill with your original inquiry and work. Your research question(s) are the areas of inquiry that you are seeking to answer with the data you will collect. There are multiple ways to approach research questions – to be discussed in detail in this chapter. In some ways, we can consider research questions to be like lesson objectives, in that they provide the focus for our inquiry. Even when your lesson goes in directions you did not anticipate, you must still remain accountable to your lesson objectives. In the same way, it is important that throughout the research process, you remain accountable to your research questions. You might even write them in big letters on a piece of paper or on your computer to always remind yourself what should serve as the focus of your process of inquiry.

Below is the overall trajectory of your research. Each step will involve particular writing components. You might consider creating a Gantt chart so that you can keep track of all phases of your research process (http://www.gantt.com/). This could assist you in both the research and writing processes.

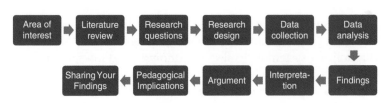

Figure 3.1 The Research Process

1. Establishing an area of interest ('topic': e.g. focus on form, interaction in asynchronous online environments)
2. Conducting a literature review (gap, state of field): peer-reviewed articles and books, blogs, documentaries, reports, other institutions' reports and materials, personal communication
3. Developing research questions (inductive/deductive)
4. Selecting an appropriate research design (methods e.g. questionnaires, interviews, focus groups, observations)

5. Data collection (e.g, piloting, sample selection)
6. Data analysis (interpretive, statistical)
7. Identification of findings
8. Interpretation of the analysis
9. Building an argument ('intended to persuade') (findings, compare to other literature)
10. Identifying implications (now what?)
11. Sharing of findings (e.g. articles, conferences, social media, reports)

As noted in Chapter 2, before identifying a research question it is important to identify the topic(s) that interest you – e.g. motivation, language choice, speaking skills (cf. Paltridge and Phakiti, 2015). This can help you to then decide what exactly you are interested in exploring. The main thing to keep in mind is that your research question(s) will need to be intimately connected with your research design. This means that your research questions are answerable with the data you plan to collect and that they are appropriate in scope to the research you are planning to do. It is also important that every term, concept and idea in your research questions is **operationalized** (given very specific definitions in your study). They should therefore be specific, **empirical** (data-based) and answerable. Below is an example of an ineffective research question, which will demonstrate the importance of these aspects:

1. 'Do students respond well to corrective feedback?' This research question is not specific enough, since it is not clear what types of corrective feedback the teacher is interested in.
2. Also, it would be difficult to collect data to demonstrate whether or not students 'respond well'. Does this refer to what they publicly demonstrate (e.g. with facial expressions, raising their hands in class) or to their internal states (e.g. emotions, motivation)?
3. This type of research question may have some answers, but they may be more subjective (from a particular perspective) than empirical.

This research question could be improved by specifying particular aspects of it that would then make it *specific, empirical (data based)* and *answerable*. For example, 'In what ways do

beginning-level Mandarin students demonstrate their engagement when teachers recast their utterances during class?' Or,
'When teachers recast their utterances during class, do beginning-level Mandarin students disengage?' In both of these
cases, 'engagement' and 'disengage' would need to be operationalized (e.g. raising their hands in class). In subsequent
sections, we will discuss deductive and inductive approaches to
research, to provide some background on research question
construction.

Implications Question

As mentioned previously, our research questions frequently
stem from an issue in our classroom that we would like to
understand better and then change or improve. In the
previous chapter, we called these 'guiding questions', as they
may be guiding you throughout your process of inquiry.
Therefore, in addition to identifying our research questions,
we can also create 'implications questions'. (In action
research the implication questions may be the impetus for
undertaking our research in the first place.) Once we have
our research findings, we can then apply those to answer our
implications questions. For example, an implication question
might be, 'Should I use my students' L1s in the classroom?' A
corresponding (inductive) research question might be, 'How
do students respond when I use their L1s in the classroom
setting?' Only when we have gone through the 11 steps of the
research process and identified findings can we then begin to
answer our implications question, which was the original
impetus for us to engage in the research in the first place. It is
essential to remember, however, that we should not 'skip
over' conducting quality research because we are in a rush to
identify our implications. Implications are more actionable
and believable when based upon rigorous and well-done
research.

Inductive and Deductive Approaches to Research

Research, as a form of systematic inquiry, can involve open-ended and/or closed approaches. This is related to our discussion in Chapter 1 of different world views that underpin our research choices. Depending on whether you choose a more open-ended approach or a closed one, your research goals may differ.

Inductive Research

Inductive research 'involves the search for pattern from observation and the development of explanations – theories – for those patterns through series of hypotheses' (Bernard, 2011, p. 7). Inductive research is sometimes called 'grounded theory building' or 'bottom-up' research. In grounded theory, the researcher 'derives a general, abstract theory of a process, action or interaction grounded in the views of participants. This process involves using multiple stages of data collection and refinement and interrelationship of categories of information (Charmaz, 2006; Corbin and Strauss, 2007)' (Creswell, 2014, p. 14).

This is an open-ended research approach that allows you to begin with topics or areas of inquiry that you are hoping to explore and then move to data collection, observation, pattern finding and ultimately findings (RESEARCH → THEORY). This type of research is emergent, meaning that it allows you to leave yourself open to unexpected (and sometimes surprising) findings that you may not have been able to predict. Inductive research questions (e.g. in ethnography, to be discussed in Chapter 7) may change over time, because of the emergent and process-oriented nature of this type of research. Inductive research, with its focus on emergent processes, can introduce a range of ethical issues related to consent, participation and observation because not all aspects of the research can be planned or foreseen (see Chapter 4).

ACTIVITY 3.1

Is there a topic of interest in your classroom[1] that you would like to explore, using inductive research? What might it be?

Deductive Research

Whereas inductive research questions move from particular cases to general theories, deductive research questions move from general theories to particular cases (THEORY → RESEARCH). For an example of a research paper that uses a deductive research question and design, see James (2010). This frequently is focused on testing hypotheses, meaning that deductive research questions are really research hypotheses. The focus is on creating hypotheses about your area of inquiry that can then be 'tested' based on the data you eventually collect. This also involves the selection of **variables**: the phenomena of interest in your study. These phenomena must be observable and measurable, and they can come in the form of *independent, dependent, intervening, moderator, control* and *extraneous* variables (http://linguistics.byu.edu/faculty/henrichsenl/ResearchMethods/RM_2_14.html). An independent variable is what is changed in the experiment. A dependent variable is affected by the changes you make to the independent variable. As you may be able to tell, deductive research can frequently control the situation in some way. This can introduce a different set of ethical considerations than those in inductive research (see Chapter 4). An example of an inductive research question would be the following: 'In what

---

1 When I write 'your classroom', you can understand that to mean a classroom in which you are the primary teacher, in which you are completing your practicum hours, or in which you are observing/involved as part of your educational programme. You can engage in inquiry in any classroom in which you participate.

ways do students experience group work in my intermediate-level reading class?' A corresponding deductive research question on the same topic might be, 'Do the lower proficiency students in my intermediate-level reading class learn more through group work than do the higher proficiency students?' You can see how the ways the question is asked will affect the research design and the eventual conclusions you can draw from the data collection and analysis.

Null and Alternative Hypotheses

When you work with quantitative data, it is essential that you identify your null and alternative hypotheses. The null hypothesis is a hypothesis of 'no difference' between two groups under study (it is the opposite of the hypothesis you are trying to test). The alternative hypothesis is that there is a difference between the two groups. A type 1 error is the false rejection of the null hypothesis, while a type 2 error is the false acceptance of the null hypothesis. These will be discussed in further detail in Chapter 11, on approaches to analysis of quantitative data.

ACTIVITY 3.2

Is there a topic of interest in your own classroom that you would like to explore using deductive research? What might it be?

Inductive Research Questions

These research questions generally begin with 'How' or 'In what ways', which does not put constraints on the research before you start. The design of the research question therefore reflects the open-ended, emergent nature of the research process itself.

You will be open to patterns that make themselves known, as opposed to deciding in advance what your variables of interest will be (as in deductive research). For inductive research design, you will start with a focus on particular topics, concepts, and issues that you will be attentive to, as opposed to any specific hypotheses you are attempting to test or variables you have identified. You should still identify specific research questions that you can easily articulate. Effective words to start inductive research questions include 'In what ways', 'In what ways, if any', 'How'; and effective words to demonstrate a potential relationship are affect, influence and impact.

ACTIVITY 3.3

Use the following framework to create a research question for your classroom. An example is provided for you.

Topics of Interest
Inductive Research Question
Operationalized Components

Example

Topics of Interest:
Generation 1.5 students, identity, peer review

Research Question

In what ways, if any, do generation 1.5 students display their identities during in-class peer-review sessions?

Operationalized Components:

generation 1.5 students, identities, display of identities, peer, peer-review sessions

In this research, interesting patterns may emerge about identities, peer interactions and the particular student group of interest (which could not have necessarily been predicted if the researcher had instead chosen a more deductive approach).

Deductive Research Questions

Deductive research questions frequently involve the creation of a testable hypothesis. Some deductive questions may start with 'Do' or 'Does', therefore asking yes-no questions that can be confirmed or disconfirmed based on the data that is collected. In other cases, they may start with 'What', leaving the research somewhat more open-ended while still involving hypotheses and variables. An example of such a research question can be found below.

ACTIVITY 3.4

Use the following framework to create a deductive research question for your classroom. An example is provided for you.

Topics of Interest
Deductive Research Question
Operationalized Components
Theory
Testable Hypothesis
Conclusion that can be drawn from a testable hypothesis

Example

Topics of Interest:
Language choice, motivation and heritage users

Deductive Research Question

What effect does an English-only classroom language policy have on Spanish heritage users' motivation?

Operationalized Components

English-only
English-only classroom language policy

Spanish heritage users
Motivation

Theory

When teachers create and enforce an English-only classroom language policy, students who are heritage users of another language will feel demotivated and therefore disengaged from classroom interaction.

Testable Hypothesis

When English teachers have 'English-only' signage in class and frequently reprimand students for using a language other than English, those students will speak less than their fellow classmates.

In deductive research, the data you collect will confirm or disconfirm your hypothesis. At that point, your argument will be based upon what your data has shown you and how it relates to the theory/hypothesis you started with.

Deductive–Inductive Hybrid Research Design

It is important to recognize that deductive and inductive research approaches can be complementary. It is possible to create a research design that includes both deductive and inductive elements. For example, you may begin with a hypothesis about an issue of interest and then test it (using a deductive approach). Once you have more information about the topic and your hypothesis, then you might start the grounded theory building process and create an inductive trajectory that is more open-ended. It is also possible that you would start with a more open-ended inductive approach and then narrow down to a theory or hypothesis, which you would then test (confirm/disconfirm) in a more traditionally deductive way. Inductive and deductive approaches are a continuum, and you should select the framework that is most useful to you and fits your interests and eventual data collection. As noted above, it is important to use a variety of different data collection methods in ways that fit the goals of your research questions.

Selecting Appropriate Data Collection Methods

Once you have settled upon a research approach, you can then begin to think about your data collection methods. One thing to keep in mind is that you can select from your methodological toolkit, from both experimental and naturalistic approaches in ways that are most appropriate and fitting in terms of answering your research questions. Each data collection method has its own **affordances** (opportunities and constraints), so it is important to consider exactly what you want to use, how you want to use it and why it fits with your particular research goals.

A good first question to ask yourself is whether you will collect data in one way or in multiple ways. For example, will you only interview students or also observe them? Will you collect experimental data that results in quantitative results as well? Next you must consider what the pros and cons of each method of data collection and data analysis (discussed in turn in the chapters that follow). What more will be added to your understanding of your topics of interest if you add additional data collection methods? Will additional methods be redundant or complementary? Ideally, you will use at least two different data collection methods so that you can begin to **triangulate** (compare and contrast) the information you learn through each.

One way to conceptualize different data collection methods is to assess whether they will provide you with information about the what, how, or why of the phenomena you are interested in (see more about this typology in Chapter 7). You could start with questionnaires for a larger sample that focus more on 'what' (information), which could be followed up by interviews and focus groups with fewer participants that would add in-depth 'how' (circumstances, conditions) and 'why' (interpretation) information. Some methods may focus more on ideologies, or belief systems and reports of behaviour (e.g. questionnaires, interviews), while others may provide more information about practices and behaviours (e.g. ethnography, observation). In your research design, you can therefore consider what combinations of research methods might work best for your research goals. Creating your research design means identifying the who, what, where, when, why and how of your methods for data collection, analysis and interpretation. It also means identifying multiple reasonable back-up plans, to increase the likelihood that you can conduct the research in a sound way.

It is important in your planning process that you consider the various ways to ensure research soundness. Generalizability is an important goal for all research, such that the ideas, concepts and phenomena you are exploring are of interest to a wide range of audiences. Additional areas of research soundness include reliability, validity and replicability especially for quantitative data (discussed in further detail in Chapter 10). For qualitative data, one can consider the importance of member checking, in which you as the researcher talk with the research participants to check your understanding and clarify questions you have about the data (http://www.qualres.org/HomeMemb-3696.html), in addition to observer agreement and triangulation (Bailey, personal communication).

Naturalistic Inquiry

Inductive research, since it is open-ended and is not focused on testing hypotheses, is frequently connected to naturalistic inquiry (nonexperimental data collection, qualitative data results and interpretive analysis methods). Nonexperimental data collection that results in qualitative data is frequently analysed in an interpretive way in order to gain an in-depth understanding of a phenomenon. Analysis is 'the search for patterns in data and for ideas that help explain why those patterns are there in the first place' (Bernard, 2011, p. 338). Researchers acknowledge that naturalistic inquiry is subjective, coming from a particular set of perspectives. This process involves the researcher's acknowledging their **positionality** during the research process (see Jansen and Peshkin in LeCompte et al. (1992) for subjectivity in qualitative research; Bernard 2011, p. 18 for a short discussion of 'trained subjectivity'). As noted in Mills and Birks (2014), 'a generally accepted tenant [sic] of qualitative research is that the researcher is an instrument (Creswell, 2013; Janesick, 2004: Merriam, 2009; Stake, 2010) who can both collect and generate data, depending on how they position themselves' (p. 32). This means that you acknowledge your own perspectives and identities as you approach your research, in order to highlight how those may have an impact on your findings. Examples of nonexperimental data collection methods are ethnography, questionnaires, observations and interviews (to be discussed in various other chapters). Some examples of nonexperimental data that can be described and analysed, depending upon your main purposes, are behaviours, events, institutions, appearance, research events (e.g. classroom activities), personal **narratives** or accounts, talk and visual records or documents (Holliday, 2015). In analysing qualitative data, it is important to ensure validity and trustworthiness in your interpretations, as they can frequently be critiqued for being overly subjective. In interpretive data analysis you may engage in the coding and memoing process, in which you search for themes and go back to your data for clear examples in order to build your argument. In qualitative data analysis it is important to consider issues of dependability, confirmability, credibility and transferability (Brown 2004, p. 495).

Psychometric Inquiry

Deductive research is frequently (though not always) connected to psychometric inquiry (experimental data collection methods, quantitative data, statistical analysis). Psychometric inquiry is generally considered more objective in nature. In research with quantitative data, objective measurement is the focus. The three types of quantitative data are nominal, ordinal and interval (Dörnyei, 2007, as cited in Phakiti, p. 32). Nominal (or categorical) data are used for 'classification and group comparison purposes' (p. 32), such as native or non-native speakers of a language; ordinal (or rank-ordered) data include Likert scale data; interval data are measured on an interval scale 'in which the distance between any two adjacent units of measurement is the same' (p. 33). In analysing quantitative data you can create tallies and percentages, descriptive statistics (e.g. mean, median, mode), or inferential statistics (e.g. T-tests, Pearson's R), in many cases using online tools to assist with the process.

Mixed Methods

As mentioned above, your methods are part of a toolkit, and you can select which tools are most fitting for a particular job. This may mean that you would mix interpretive and statistical analysis of quantitative and qualitative data (see Ivankova and Greer, 2015; Creswell and Plano Clark, 2010). This could involve concurrent quantitative and qualitative data collection and analysis, sequential quantitative-qualitative, or sequential qualitative-quantitative (Ivankova and Greer, 2015, p. 69). Mixed methods research allows you to see the phenomena of interest from a range of perspectives, and therefore your findings can be considered more robust and rigorous.

ACTIVITY 3.5

Create an inductive research question and a deductive research question about a topic in your school that interests you. How do the questions differ? Would you collect data differently for each of the research questions? If so, how?

ACTIVITY 3.6

Select two elements in your classroom – how could you approach a study of the relationship between the two of them using an inductive approach? How about a deductive approach?

Pedagogical Implications

After constructing research questions, collecting data and ultimately conceptualizing your argument, you can determine what this will mean for your teaching (your pedagogical implications). These pedagogical implications may be at the macro level or micro level. For example, depending on what you discover, you might start planning your lessons differently. Or you might engage in different classroom practices. Or you might take on a different disposition towards particular students (or types of students). This will give you an opportunity to consider how your findings can ultimately shape your practices and ideologies as they relate to your pedagogy. In conceptualizing your research questions, it is important to keep in mind the range of possible ways in which what you discover could affect your eventual classroom practice.

Conclusion

As you move from your topic of interest to your research question to your research design, you will be engaging in a series of important decisions. Continue reading the literature to have a good sense of how other researchers have approached their methods for topics similar to yours, as this is central to the design of an effective research project. Also keep in mind that your research question may shift over time (e.g. to a different focus, to a smaller set of issues), so it is important to remain flexible throughout the process so that you can focus your inquiry on both the issues that interest you and those that are emerging.

Suggested Readings

http://twp.duke.edu/uploads/media_items/research-questions.
original.pdf

This straightforward resource provides you with detailed
information about inductive and deductive research questions,
along with key examples.

www.maxwell.syr.edu/moynihan/cqrm/Qualitative_Methods_
Newsletters/Qualitative_Methods_Newsletters/

This series of newsletters from Syracuse University's Center on
Qualitative and Multi-Method Inquiry can give you ongoing and
up-to-date information about various forms of naturalistic and
mixed methods research.

http://catalogue.flatworldknowledge.com/bookhub/reader
/3585?e=blackstone_1.0-ch02_s03#blackstone_1.0-ch00about

http://www.blackwellreference.com/public/tocnode?id=g978140
5124331_chunk_g978140512433120_ss1–6

Principles of Sociological Inquiry, by Amy Blackstone, includes relevant
information about all stages of research (including research ethics,
research design and defining and measuring concepts) (you need to
create an account to access the entire website).

http://research-methodology.net/research-methodology/research-
types/

This clear and accessible resource provides useful frameworks
and examples especially suited for those who are newer to the
research enterprise.

Research Ethics: Reasons, Roles, Responsibilities and Relationships

Guiding Questions:

1. What is your definition of ethics?
2. Where does your definition come from?
3. Can you identify an ethical dilemma you have faced in your professional practice in the past month?
4. How did you handle it?
5. What might you have done differently? Why?

Introduction

This chapter will discuss the 4 R's of ethical issues raised by research: reasons, roles, responsibilities and relationships at the personal and institutional levels. In particular, the chapter will discuss the management of roles and perspectives, informed consent, boundaries, power, bias and exploitation. It will highlight how a teacher's identities and others' perceptions can shape the material one can reasonably attain. In addition, it will emphasize the ethical dilemmas involved in taking on a researcher role to analysing data that may have originally been shared for educational purposes when one was in a teacher role. It will also provide strategies for you as a researcher for approaching your students and other stakeholders and asking them to provide data (e.g. interviews).

A useful distinction in relation to ethics comes from the field of psychology (Jordan and Meara, 1990): principle ethics vs virtue ethics. Principle ethics emphasize the use of objective, rational standards, rules, or universal codes in determining an ethical judgement (e.g, professional ethics codes). Examples of professional ethics code may come from different fields (https://lsaethics.wordpress.com, http://ethics.americananthro.org/about). Virtue ethics emphasizes the use of historical 'virtues' and the development of an individual's character and focuses on character traits. Principle ethics therefore asks, 'What shall I do?', whereas virtue ethics asks, 'Who shall I be?'

Ethics: Definitions

Research ethics (cf. Creswell, 2014; DeCosta, 2015a; DeCosta, 2015b; Hesse-Biber and Leavy, 2011; Kimmel, 1988; Israel and Hay, 2006; Fine, 1993; Punch, 2005; Sieber, 1998) is appropriate context-dependent conduct that demonstrates a sensitivity to reasons, roles, responsibilities and relationships (the 4 R's). For a discussion of ethics for qualitative researchers in education, see Deyhle, Hess and LeCompte, pp. 597–642 in LeCompte et al., 1992. As Creswell (2014) highlights that 'ethical questions are apparent today in such issues as personal disclosure, authenticity, and credibility of the research report; the role of researchers in cross-cultural contexts; and issues of personal privacy through forms of Internet data collection (Israel and Hay, 2006)' (p. 92).

'Reasons' here means your goals, aims and objectives in conducting the research: Why are you doing the research? Whom is the research for? To what ends will it be used? 'Roles' means the subject positions that you and your research participants may occupy over the course of the research. For example, will your role be primarily researcher or teacher? Will their roles be primarily students or research subjects? Is it clear to everyone involved what everyone's roles are and how those roles may shift/change over time? 'Responsibilities' means the tasks/duties involved in your various roles. This involves a sensitivity to power differentials and also to the avoidance of exploitation or coercion. 'Relationships' are built through ongoing interactions among those involved in the research enterprise and can shift depending on the various roles one takes on. For all 4 R's, the notion of boundaries is important – those 'lines in the sand' that distinguish all of the individuals and groups involved in the research enterprise – it is important that there be mechanisms in place so that these boundaries can be negotiated upfront and in an ongoing way so that they remain transparent to everyone engaged in the research.

Ethics throughout the Research Process

It is important to recognize that ethical issues may arise at any stage of the research process, which are specific to the particular tasks and activities that you are involved in at that phase (see table 4.1 pp. 93–94 in Creswell 2014 for a summary of ethical issues in quantitative, qualitative and mixed methods research during various phases of the research process). These include planning the research (e.g. informing participants far enough in advance), data collection (e.g. which participants to include), data analysis (e.g. coding the data in ways that faithfully represent the details of the data) and sharing of findings (e.g. how you describe the research to different audiences). The idea of perspective-taking – that is, imagining what each member of the research enterprise understands about and contributes to the research itself (including the researcher, the researched and the research readers) – should permeate your approach to ethics at all stages of research. This includes developing ethical strategies for approaching and explaining your research to potential participants. Bailey (2007, p. 15) highlights the relevance of three primary ethical issues: informed consent, deception and confidentiality.

ACTIVITY 4.1

Select a phase of the research process and identify at least five ethical issues that may arise during that phase. What might you do to mitigate the ethical problems that may surface during the phase that you identified?

Ethics of Different Data Collection Methods

In addition to recognizing the range of ethical issues possible at each stage of the research process, one can also think through the ethics of different data collection methods. Each research method that we will discuss has particular ethical issues associated with it. In action research we frequently have in mind in advance how our findings might be used in our classrooms. This means that we sometimes consider our implication questions before fully going through the process of inquiry as it relates to our research questions. This can sometimes get us into unethical territory, as some might question whether we are biased in the ways that we have analysed our data. It is important to consider all of these potential issues in advance and mitigate them if possible. There will inevitably be ethical issues you encounter throughout the process that could not have been predicted, but your having thought through at least some of these details in advance will facilitate the overall process. Being part of a community of practice as you engage in inquiry will also help you with research ethics, as you can discuss ethical dilemmas and questions with other teachers and researchers. They can help you think through potential courses of action, based on their own previous experiences, the experiences of colleagues whom they know and/or examples they have read in the literature.

For example, what are some of the ethical issues involved in observations? It is important to acknowledge that observations are never neutral information-collection procedures but are instead subjective approaches intended to gain a particular set of perspectives in a specific context. For example, what would you do if you were observing a colleague for your research and they said something inappropriate to a student? If you were to take your researcher role as primary, then you might not say anything. But if you were to take your teacher role as primary, then you might talk with your colleague afterwards, asking questions about the lesson, the student and the particulars of the context. Or what would you do if you notice during a classroom observation in another classroom that two students are fighting throughout the lesson? As a fellow teacher, you may feel the need to reprimand or control the students' behaviour. However, in your primary role as researcher, it may not be appropriate for you to 'affect the scene' through intervening in a classroom management issue. This would be something to consider in advance and also discuss with anyone whom you will be observing for your research if questions arise throughout the research process.

How about the research ethics of questionnaires? As part of the process of creating a questionnaire we will design the 'questionnaire description', the paragraph that explains the questionnaire and its purpose to the potential respondents. It is important that the questionnaire description incorporate all possible purposes in advance so that you are as transparent as possible with the respondents. For example, are you planning to use an excerpt from an open-ended questionnaire response in a presentation to your local school board? If so, then that information needs to be shared with the respondents in advance. Respondents respond to questionnaires in ways that are shaped by the potential audiences for whom it will be used. Therefore, it is our job as the researcher to predict the various uses of our work. If we imagine that we might use the data for a particular purpose, then we need to let our participants know this and give them the option of 'opting out' for particular modes (without feeling coerced to 'opt in' to everything).

And the ethics of video-recording? In educational institutions' institutional review board processes, you would need to

won't that skew the research?

have research participants complete an informed consent form, in which you would give them the opportunity to opt in or out of being video-recorded or having their image shown in conference presentations (for example). It is essential that we treat our research subjects with respect and ensure that they are aware of the ways they are studied by us as well as represented to others.

In some types of experimental research you provide interventions (e.g. additional computer time) to one group but not to the control group, in order to investigate the potential effects of that intervention on the students. If the research finds that additional computer time enhances language learning, then was it ethical to not also provide that additional time to the other group of students? Are there some interventions that seem appropriate and others that may seem less ethical?

Before engaging in a particular data collection method, you should reflect on the possible ethical issues that may arise. While it is impossible to predict every possible issue and also impossible to get rid of all negative consequences associated with them, it is important to create a plan for how you might think through and mitigate the effects of those ethical issues.

ACTIVITY 4.2

Select a data collection method that you believe you would use in your own research. Create a list of five possible ethical issues of that data collection method. How might you mitigate these ethical issues?

Dual Roles and Dual Relationships

Action research is 'a form of enquiry that enables practitioners everywhere to investigate and evaluate their work' (McNiff and Whitehead, 2006, p. 7). In action research, you could be conducting research in your own classroom with the intention of making pedagogical changes based upon what you find (cf. Wallace, 1998), which automatically involves your taking on dual roles. On the one hand, this may seem like a good thing because you are able to build on existing relationships in your creation of a research undertaking. However, having dual roles can also create **conflicts of interest**, in which decisions are made from the perspective of (and benefit of) one of those roles but to the detriment of a relationship. For example, when you are meeting with students to explain to them a research project you are interested in doing, they may perceive that their agreeing (or not agreeing) to participate in the research may have a (positive or negative) effect on their grade. In a case like this, the decisions you make in your role as researcher may have a bearing on decisions you make in your role as teacher. In order to avoid such dilemmas one might then be tempted to not ask the students whether or not they want to be involved in the research. But this would be an example of how one's researcher role is creating a situation in which research participants are not fully knowledgeable about the purposes and goals of the research. Therefore, you should do your best to make it clear to your students that their being involved in the research is entirely voluntary and has no bearing on the grade, and you should ensure that you make yourself available to answer individual and group questions they may have about the research process.

Ethical Dilemmas

Ethical dilemmas involve your questioning what the most appropriate course of action would be, in order to minimize the harm that might be done to anyone involved in the research enterprise. Dilemmas may come during data collection or data sharing, for example. A data collection dilemma might come about in deductive research when you provide a resource (e.g. additional time with a particular technology) to one group of students instead of another. This technology time may have a positive effect on only one group's learning, but how can you reasonably measure that effect without conducting the research in the ways that you have planned? Or a data sharing dilemma may arise when you consider whom you want to share your research with (e.g. students themselves, their parents, school administrators) – will you share exactly the same version in every case? Does a sensitivity to audience design actually involve picking and choosing which aspects of the research you will share, and how? When you encounter an ethical dilemma what are the steps in how you handle it? At first this may involve negotiating with yourself and asking yourself, What are the issues involved? What are my roles and responsibilities, and how might these have a bearing on my relationships? How then do you communicate with others who are involved in your ethical dilemma? Ethical dilemmas are pervasive in research, and the most important thing is to be honest with yourself and everyone involved in the research enterprise, to make sure you are conducting yourself in the most ethical way possible.

Researcher Perspectives

One researcher whom I spoke to about ethical dilemmas described a collaborative research project that was going in a direction that he was increasingly uncomfortable with. After concluding the project, he noted that 'Moving forward, I have promised to myself that I will never do research ... that blames participants for not doing something that I or my colleagues, based on our interests and biases, think they should be doing.' The notion of perspective-taking, in understanding our research participants, was key in this situation.

Another researcher, engaged in action research in his own classroom, had dilemmas about his course design as it related to his research interests. He asked himself, 'Am I making these choices because they will make my research life easier or because they are the most sound pedagogical choices?' Action research, because of your multiple roles, can introduce these dilemmas. Therefore, it is important to be critically reflective throughout the research process in order to ensure ethical practice in relation to your own work and that of your students.

Institutional Review Board

At many higher education institutions (especially in the United States), there are institutional review boards (IRB) that review the research of faculty and students at that institution. They ensure that all research plans are ethical and adhere to protocols intended to protect the research participant (as well as the institution). It is essential that you find out about the process at your institution before engaging in research of any kind (even small-scale research). It is possible that your research would satisfy the exempt categories or the 'expedited review' categories. But, it is vital that you proceed through the relevant steps in order to ensure that you are engaging in ethical practice and that your research participants' perspectives are the top priority. In particular, the IRB may have you explain in detail how you will ensure four key components of ethical research: confidentiality, right to privacy, anonymity and pseudonyms (Phakiti, p. 42).

Cultural and Linguistic Aspects of Ethics

When considering how you might approach ethics in your research, it is also essential to recognize the cultural and linguistic aspects. For example, will your students (as language learners) understand all that you are asking of them in the research? And cultural awareness in ethics is crucial. For example, how do notions of authority, respect and politeness play a role in whether or not a potential research participant perceives whether or not they can truly say no to you?

Furthermore, what might happen if you are interested in exploring the views of non-literate participants but your consent form is in written form? How might you ensure their understanding without compromising the integrity of your project? Though it is not possible to create a research project that is ethically perfect, it is important to recognize and address these issues throughout the process.

ACTIVITY 4.3

Brainstorm how you would explain your research to a beginner-level language learner. How will you make sure that they have understood what you are doing and what their roles are? What if their parent wants to have a better understanding of the research you are planning to do. How would you explain the research to them?

ACTIVITY 4.4

Read a published study in applied linguistics. What were the ethical issues? How were they addressed? Are there any ethical issues that were not addressed in the publication? If you were conducting this research, how might you plan for and handle similar ethical issues?

Conclusion

Research ethics involves an ongoing sensitivity to reasons, roles, responsibilities and relationships. It is essential to consider ethical issues throughout the research process, and for particular aspects of your research design. Being part of a supportive community of practice can help to ensure that you engage in research that adheres to both personal and institutional ethical standards.

Suggested Readings

http://www.qualitative-research.net/index.php/fqs/article/
view/572/1241
In this (2004) issue of Qualitative Research Forum, authors
Marshall and Batten highlight the cross-cultural ethical issues
related to research design and implementation.

http://www.socialresearchmethods.net/kb/ethics.php
In this section on 'Ethics in Research' from the Web Center for
Social Research Methods you can learn about key concepts in
ethics, with clear definitions of each.

Morton, A. (1999). 'Ethics in Action Research'. Systemic Practice and
Action Research Volume 12(2): pp. 219–222.
This helpful article provides an overview of ethical issues to
consider in engaging in research, and specific issues to keep in
mind when doing action research.

Mills, G.E. (2000). *Action Research: A Guide for the Teacher Researcher.*
http://eric.ed.gov/?id=ED439152
This comprehensive guide provides teacher researchers with a
detailed approach to all aspects of the action research enterprise.
It also includes a useful in-depth case study as well as online
resources for action researchers.

Action Research and The Implications for Ethics in Human Research
https://www.csu.edu.au/research/ethics_safety/human/
ehrc_actnres
This online resource provides a concise set of definitions and
issues to consider when engaging in action research, along with
useful resources for further exploration.

Section II: Data Collection

5

Making Questionnaires Work for You

Guiding Questions:

1. Do you believe questionnaire data when you hear about it in the media? Why? Why not?
2. Have you ever taken a questionnaire before, for any purpose?
3. What was your experience like?
4. What aspects of the questionnaire did you like/not like?
5. What are some of the pros and cons of using questionnaires to collect data?

Introduction

This chapter provides an overview of effective questionnaire design, for a range of different purposes in your research. It discusses the possibilities for questionnaires (e.g. collecting a lot of data quickly) and limitations (e.g. depending on only what people say they believe and/or do). In particular, the chapter highlights the questionnaire process, from the macro level (organization) to the micro level (word choice). In addition, it provides details about questionnaire design, including the range of question types and their positives and negatives, as well as the order of questions. It focuses on if we should ask demographic questions and if so, how and where. The chapter also provides tools for effective question design (cf. Boyd and Heritage, 2006; Clayman and Heritage,

2002), acknowledging that the ways that questions are constructed has a large impact on the responses that will be shared. The chapter also include details of online tools (e.g. Google Docs, SurveyMonkey) for collecting questionnaire data. Lastly, Chapter 5 provides key questions to think about in relation to using questionnaire data in combination with other data collection methods like interviews and discourse analysis. This chapter goes into depth on all of these topics, because much of what we discuss here can be applied in some way to other research methods we will discuss in other chapters.

It is important to recognize that every method you choose has a range of affordances (possibilities and constraints). In considering which method to employ for your research, you can weigh what you see as the pros and the cons of that particular method as it relates to your particular research question. Below is a matrix that provides information about the methods that are discussed in Chapters 5 and 6. 'Asynchronous' means that the data is collected in such a way that the researcher and the participant are not interacting with one another at the same time. For example, when you provide someone with a questionnaire, they may fill it out, and then you as the audience read it at another time. 'Synchronous' means that the researcher and the participant(s) interact at the same time. For example, when you are interviewing someone, you interact with them in real time (though you may analyse the interview transcripts later).

Synchronous methods allow for more back-and-forth between participants, which means that you as the researcher can clarify and expand on the participants' contributions during interactions with the research participants. Asynchronous methods, on the other hand, involve the researcher's creating very clear questions and explanations since the respondents do not generally have an opportunity to interact with the researcher face to face. If you are concerned about your research participants' understanding your questionnaire,

Table 5.1 Affordances of Questionnaires, Interviews, Focus Groups and Reflections

Method	Interaction type	Participants involved at any one time	Additional information
Questionnaires	Asynchronous	One Participant	Researcher collects multiple questionnaires from different individuals
Interviews	Synchronous	Researcher(s) & One Participant	Researcher collects multiple interviews from different individuals
Focus Groups	Synchronous	Researcher & Multiple Participants	Researcher may engage in one or multiple focus groups
Reflections	Synchronous or Asynchronous	Various Possibilities	Researcher collects multiple reflections

however, you can provide them with opportunities to ask clarifying questions while they are completing them.

Why Use Questionnaires?

Surveys are a process of gathering information that is generalizable from a particular sample (Fowler, 2009) and are pervasive in applied linguistics research (Wagner, 2015). Survey data can be collected through questionnaires, a survey research instrument that they can yield both qualitative and quantitative data (e.g. for needs assessments and pre- and post-assessments). They can be used to collect data about (for example) individuals' and groups' ideologies, belief systems and values; reports of behaviour; self-assessments of ability; or evaluation of activities. Though some researchers may believe that designing a good questionnaire is easy, it can be quite difficult, especially since your eventual goal is to collect and analyse data that is truly representative of individuals' and groups' realities (cf. Bernard, 2011, pp. 187–222).

We will here discuss questionnaires in great detail since some of their features are generalizable to other types of research methods. Questionnaires have a number of affordances, including the fact that you can collect a lot of data efficiently and that the data can be easily compared. However, they also have limitations, primarily based on the fact that you are depending on only what people say they believe and/ or do. This is one reason why questionnaires can be most effective when paired with other data collection methods (e.g. interviews, observations). In addition, it is important to keep in mind that individuals share information partially, based on what they perceive as the reasons, roles, responsibilities and relationships associated with the research (see Chapter 4 on ethics). Therefore, there are limits to the type of information that we can reasonably collect through questionnaire data. Furthermore, in relation to the pervasive question about whether one can believe what people say in questionnaires, we can simply acknowledge that questionnaires can capture only a certain kind of data. This takes the pressure off of questionnaire data being a 'truly accurate' picture of what people really believe and/or do.

Empathy and the Psychology of Questionnaire Responses

An essential aspect of effective questionnaire design is empathy, or perspective-taking. Since questionnaires are an asynchronous method of data collection, it is important that you consistently imagine how its organization, purpose and questions might be perceived by the potential respondents. **Piloting** (i.e. giving a draft of the questionnaire to individuals so that they can provide you with feedback) can help in this endeavour, and it is important that it be incorporated into all of your decisions as you create your questionnaire.

Before beginning to make decisions about the macro- and micro-level organization of your questionnaire, it is important to keep in mind the psychology of responding to questionnaires, highlighted in Johnson (2011). There are five steps that respondents must go through when they answer your questions (Johnson, 2011):

1. encoding and storage (of information sought)
2. comprehension of question
3. retrieval of information
4. judgement and estimation
5. reporting an answer

Recognizing these multiple steps helps us to acknowledge that respondents' answers are a *version* of the truth, as reported through the prism of an individual's perceptions.

In addition, respondents may have problems when they respond to questions (Johnson, 2011):

1. failure to encode information sought
2. misinterpretation of questions
3. forgetting & other memory problems
4. flawed judgement or estimation strategies
5. problems in formatting answer
6. deliberate misreporting
7. failure to follow instructions

These issues should inform our approach to questionnaire design, collection and analysis, as they help to underscore the human element inherent in collecting data of this kind.

Key Issues in Questionnaire Design

Before considering how you will design the questionnaire itself, it is important to ask yourself some key questions about the process. These include big questions like your focal population and sampling or whether or not you will compensate the participants (Schuh & Associates, 2008):

1. What do you want to measure?
2. Population & Sampling?
3. Sample size?
4. Used once or more than once?
5. Instrument type?
6. Piloting?
7. Timeline?
8. Survey Delivery?
9. Compensation?

ACTIVITY 5.1

Go through the list of nine issues above in relation to a questionnaire that you plan to distribute to your students. What additional questions about the process do you have at this point? Keep track of these questions as you read the rest of the chapter.

How Do I Put Together the Questionnaire?

This section will highlight the questionnaire process and design, from the macro level (organization) to the micro level (word choice). The first thing to think about in constructing your questionnaire is clarity. Since questionnaires are generally asynchronous, you want to be sure that your questions (and the intentions behind them) are as clear as possible to the respondents. You also want to keep in mind the important goal of mitigating bias in the order of questions, whether all of the questions are required or optional (or which questions are required vs optional), which demographic questions you ask and the question design itself. Another issue to address is how long the questionnaire will be. You want to make sure that participants respond to the questionnaire (and the whole questionnaire), and a big part of this is their perception of how long it will take them to complete it. The next consideration is the range of question types (including demographic questions). You can also determine what order to put the questions in, based on whether you think this will encourage/discourage them to complete the questionnaire. As noted above, it is essential to take the respondents' perspective into account when making decisions about the questionnaire.

Macro-Level Issues

There are a number of macro-level issues to consider when creating your questionnaire, all of which relate back to empathy. Make sure that you consistently think about your questionnaire from the perspective of your respondents.

Questionnaires are a genre and therefore have particular features associated with them. There is a certain set of possible organizational structures as well. For the respondents, it should make sense why you are asking questions in the order you are asking them (e.g. that the different information you ask for has clear connections to the other information you asked for). Generally speaking, I would recommend putting all demographic questions either at the beginning or the end of the questionnaire. If you put them at the beginning, the respondent might start wondering about what you are really interested in, which could potentially bias their responses in some way. If you are concerned about this, then you could put the demographic questions at the end. I would also recommend including questions that are 'easier to answer' (e.g. dichotomous, ranking) earlier in the questionnaire, with more open-ended questions (and those dichotomous and ranking questions that ask for elaboration) later in the questionnaire. In a sense, these first questions serve as '**schema activation**' (just like in a good lesson), which can then give you more in-depth and thoughtful responses once those open-ended questions come towards the end.

One important issue to keep in mind, however, is that you do not want to the respondents to believe that the entire questionnaire comprises only dichotomous and ranking questions. If they believe so, then they may get frustrated with having to answer more in-depth questions at the end if they are not expecting them. You may therefore wish to include information about the question types in the short description of the questionnaire that you include at the top. This choice would mean that you have kept in mind the perspectives of your participants as you engage in the questionnaire design process. And it is important to strike the right balance among various question types and their order in your questionnaires. Below are some guidelines (Johnson, 2011), some of which we will discuss in further detail:

A. questions ordered to seem logical
B. first questions should be relevant & easy
C. most salient to least salient for your research interests
D. no demographic questions at beginning
E. group similar items together
F. potentially objectionable questions placed near the end
G. place instructions where they are needed

Formatting Tips:

H. use larger font, colours, spacing to attract attention, show groupings
I. symbols to identify starting point
J. number questions consecutively
K. consistent background
L. questions in bold & answer responses in lighter font

All of the guidelines above are for the benefit of the respondent, and they will help you organize your data during the analysis process. Point B highlights the fact that you do not want to discourage your respondents by giving them difficult questions at the very beginning, but this should be balanced with including questions at the beginning that are salient for your research questions. It is important to keep the respondents motivated since they are frequently anonymous and may therefore feel little reason to complete the entire questionnaire.

Putting demographic questions at the end means that participants will be less likely to guess what your 'true' research interests are and then respond accordingly. Putting potentially objectionable questions at the end also connects with the rapport you have with the individual (outside of class and in the questionnaire itself), so that they may be more willing to respond to your questions towards the end. The best questionnaires have a 'rhythm' to them that acknowledges what the experience of completing the questionnaire might feel like to different participants. The formatting tips that are provided are especially useful for language learners since the tips are a form of *modified input* (Long, 1982), language that learners are exposed to that is adapted for them, which can encourage language learners to complete the questionnaire. In addition, one can consider that the respondents are in some sense 'primed' for more difficult questions at the end. But also make sure that you have an appropriate balance, such that there are not too many difficult questions and they then provide short answers just to finish the questionnaire.

You can also consider whether you want the questionnaire responses to be anonymous or not. It is possible that the anonymous responses and the set of responses in aggregate will be sufficiently useful to you, depending upon your research interests. However, in other cases, it may be necessary or preferable to know who exactly shared what. This is especially the case if you plan to do follow-up interviews for elaboration on questionnaire responses. You also want to weigh whether the respondents may be more or less honest if they have to include their names, and you can make their sharing their names optional. In addition, you can think about who your target population (sample) is, in terms of the types of data that will help you answer your research question(s). Participants may be more willing to divulge sensitive information in an anonymous questionnaire rather than an interview. However, one must also keep in mind that if the questionnaire is anonymous they may choose not to respond at all.

Questionnaire Description

At the beginning of your questionnaire, you will include a short description of who you are and what your interests are (in inductive research in particular, this will simply be a list of topics). You may also want to include information about how long you believe the questionnaire will take (based on what you learn from piloting your questionnaire, to be discussed below). If you have gone through an IRB process, then the information you would include here would have been vetted by the IRB of your institution. Your participants would have therefore signed an informed consent form, which outlines exactly what they are agreeing to in relation to the research. I would recommend that you include the following thirteen components in your questionnaire descriptions:

A. who you are (identities relevant to this audience)
B. purpose of the research
C. topics of interest
D. why they're receiving it/why they were selected
E. what the results may be used for (questionnaire audiences, needs, and decisions)
F. whether the data or results will be anonymous (not identifiable, e.g., pseudonyms)
G. whether the data or results will be confidential (not shared with others e.g., colleagues)
H. whether results will be aggregated
I. mode of completion
J. estimate of length of time to complete the questionnaire

K. timeline for completion
L. compensation
M. if they may be contacted for future questionnaires or other data collection
N. your contact information

It is important that your questionnaire description be clear and concise and that you include it in your piloting process. In addition, make sure that you provide clear definitions of any terminology that might be relevant for the participants to know and understand.

Questionnaire Design

Here I will provide details about questionnaire design, including the range of question types and their positives and negatives, as well as the order of questions. I will discuss if we can, how to and when to effectively ask demographic questions. It is important that all of the questions in your questionnaire directly relate back to your research question.

Demographic Questions

Generally speaking, questionnaires include demographic questions, in which you ask the respondents basic information about who they are. These questions can take the form of 'fill-in-the-blank' or 'select which of the following' type questions. The important thing to keep in mind is that the content of these questions should be closely related to the focus of your research. For example, if you are interested in finding out about students' different levels of participation in class, you may be interested in asking them their countries of origin. That information could enable you to make arguments that relate students' backgrounds and their intercultural communication skills. However, it may not be necessary to ask students' age in a case like this if your primary research interests do not have anything to do with age. But you do want to leave it open in terms of possible relationships you could draw between the demographic information about your respondents and the responses they provide. Another thing to consider is whether to put the demographic questions at the beginning or end of the questionnaire. Again, it is important to consider how your respondents may perceive your reasons for asking particular demographic questions and how this may then shape their eventual responses.

ACTIVITY 5.2

Think of a demographic issue that you are interested in for your own research. Why do you believe it is important for your research? How will you ask a question about this issue?

Question Type Selection

As mentioned previously, one of the affordances of questionnaires is that they allow you to easily compare data across respondents and questions. It is important to include a range of different question types, which fit the particular interests associated with your research question. In addition, if you plan to conduct quantitative analysis, it is important to create questions that can be analysed using nominal, ordinal, interval, or **ratio** measures (discussed further in Chapter 9).

Dichotomous Questions

Dichotomous questions include yes/no, true/false and agree/disagree questions. These may be appropriate for certain issues you want to explore (e.g., Do you use an L1 dictionary for vocabulary learning when in class?). They can also serve you well as pre-questions for more in-depth questions (e.g. How often do you use an L1 dictionary for vocabulary learning when in class? (Likert scale) and What are your perspectives on L1 dictionary use for vocabulary learning? (open-ended)). Dichotomous questions are generally the easiest to analyse and can allow respondents to first simply consider the topic at hand before afterwards diving deeper with more in-depth responses.

Ranking Questions

Ranking questions are one type of multi-response question. Ranking questions ask the respondent to rank (put in order) a range of items. These include Likert scale (e.g. very confident, confident, neutral, unconfident, very unconfident) and 'To what extent do you agree with the following statement?' and then the following response options: strongly agree, agree, neutral, disagree and strongly disagree. This question type may also involve the respondents' putting a list in order of preference (e.g. asking students to put five grammar points in order from favourite to least favourite). Since responses to ranking questions involve gradation and granularity, they can provide more nuance than can dichotomous questions. However, this can also mean that they become more complex to analyse, to be discussed in Chapter 11. Some effective ways to ask ranking questions are disagree—agree, oppose—favourable, important—not important, hardly ever—very often (with 5- or 7-point scales that include neutral). Though not all questionnaire designers agree with an odd number of points on the scale, the reality is that some respondents will feel neutral about a topic you are asking them about. Therefore, the questionnaire should include 'neutral' as an option. You might also consider including 'I don't know' or 'I'm not sure' as options, especially in cases when language learners may not fully understand the questions being asked. It is generally good practice to include (optional) open-ended options after dichotomous and Likert scale questions, as this can provide more elaboration and context for data analysis.

One important thing to keep in mind when designing questionnaires, especially for one's students, is that the questionnaire does not appear to become like a test that you would give them as their instructor. Doing this may have some unintended and affect-related consequences. This is why we do not generally include test-like (e.g. multiple choice, fill-in-the-blank) questions on research questionnaires that we give to students.

Multiple Options Questions

Multiple options questions provide respondents with a range of possible responses from which to select. One example could be 'In which of the following contexts have you interacted in your L2 with someone new? Select all that apply: The library, The bookstore, The grocery store.' Another example could be 'I feel comfortable interacting in my L2 with the following individuals: a classmate, a stranger, a professor.' These questions allow you to provide some options for the respondents, but there should always also be an 'Other, Please explain' option at the end, as well, in case you have not exhausted all relevant possibilities.

Open-Ended Questions

The last broad category of questionnaire questions is open-ended questions. These questions can provide you with more in-depth information about a particular set of issues that relate to your research question (e.g. asking respondents to share a story, respond to hypothetical scenarios, or elaborate on a dichotomous or Likert scale question). For example, perhaps you are interested in the use of synchronous sessions in a hybrid Chinese course (in particular whether or not they help to create community in the class). You could ask the students an open-ended question like 'What do you think about the synchronous sessions for this class?' This question, though perhaps difficult to analyse, could provide interesting insights that relate to your research question. These insights and their depth would not be possible if you were to ask the 'same' question as a yes/no (e.g. 'Do you like the synchronous sessions for this class?' Yes or no). Open-ended questions also allow your respondents to provide specific instances/stories, or even responses to hypothetical scenarios (to give you a sense of their general ideologies about a particular issue). Open-ended questions can also be provided in conjunction with other question types, for example by asking for elaboration/explanation after a dichotomous or ranking question.

Effective questionnaires include a range of question types, each of which is selected for the particular purposes you have in mind. Also, you may want to have multiple questions that are all getting at the same construct so that you are not depending on only one question. But too many questions about the same construct may become frustrating for respondents. Therefore, it is important to strike the right balance in this regard.

Linguistic Considerations

This section provides tools for effective question design (cf. Boyd and Heritage, 2006; Clayman and Heritage, 2002), acknowledging that the particular ways that questions are constructed has a large impact on the responses that will be shared. When considering question design, it is important to take into consideration how your questions will be understood by the respondents and to make sure that bias is mitigated. You can decide if you want to ask yes/no questions (which may include some preference for a particular type of response) or wh– questions. For example, what would be the difference between asking, 'Do you think that students should listen to TED Talks to increase their listening ability?', and asking, 'What are your thoughts on TED Talks for listening classes?' The first question invites a 'yes' response (because of its syntax and also because of the words 'increase' and 'ability', whereas the second leaves it more open to the students' interpretation.

One question we can also consider is whether our questionnaire's question design reflects best practices in the field or describes things in a way that will be understandable to the respondents. For example, would I include 'native speaker' and 'non-native speaker' in my questionnaire when in my professional practice I am more inclined to use the term 'user' (Cook, 2008)?

ACTIVITY 5.3

Determine the pros and cons of these different ways to ask demographic questions.

1. Country of origin – fill-in-blank OR
   Where are you from?
2. List the languages you know and how fluent you are OR
   List the languages you know. Rate your proficiency in these languages on the following scale (http://www.actfl.org/sites/default/files/pdfs/Can-Do_Statements_2015.pdf) OR
   List the languages you know. Rate your ability in the four skills.

ACTIVITY 5.4

Is there a topic that you might like to use a questionnaire for? Identify a few questions you might include in the questionnaire. How would you word those questions in order to best correspond to what you meant to ask?

In some cases, you may also need to consider which language(s) your questionnaire will be in and why. This may also involve translation, in which case you would need to also consider which will be the first language and which will be underneath that language. All of these small decisions can shape whether and how participants respond to the question-naire. In addition, your word choice and question design should incorporate as little bias as possible. One way to do this is to provide for the full range of possibilities, like 'To what extent do you agree **or disagree** with the following statement'. Or 'In what ways, **if any**, does your instructor increase your motiva-tion to learn this language?' In many ways, language teachers are very well equipped to create questionnaires that demon-strate a deep sensitivity to question creation and audience design, since we are so aware of the details of language-in-use.

Piloting

After you create the questionnaire, you will want to make sure that you pilot it (Creswell, 2014, p. 161) with a participant (or participants) who is/are in the population you are interested in. This means that you will have that person/those people take the questionnaire and provide honest responses to it, and then they will give you feedback on the organization, length, question order, question types and question design. Based on the feedback that you receive, you will make changes to the questionnaire, in order to maximize the likelihood that you will get the number and kind of responses you are looking for. This does not mean that every respondent will necessarily understand and accurately interpret every question, but it can help with this process. It may be the case that you will need to make additional changes to the questionnaire later in the process as well. This revision process will be an ongoing one, based on the data you are able to collect.

Questionnaire Distribution

Once you have created your questionnaire, piloted it and determined its final form, you can decide how you would like to distribute it. Just like any methodological consideration, there are pros and cons to consider. You could consider whether to give students the questionnaire in person, online (usually distributed via email) and/or through the mail.

If you are working with language learners in particular, then online tools like those described below can give students the time to process the questions and respond to them in ways that are useful for your research. You can use a tool like Google Docs (docs.google.com), which can allow you to create a questionnaire of any length with a number of different question types (along with optional 'help text' underneath each question). You need a Google account to create the questionnaire, but respondents do not need a Google account to respond to it. You also have the option of making certain questions required and other questions optional. One con to this is that it does not automatically provide question numbers with the questions. In addition, it is not possible to save responses and come back to them, which can sometimes cause issues for respondents. Google Docs automatically creates a spreadsheet, as well as visual representations, of the data, which can make it easier to analyse.

Online questionnaire creation tools (e.g. SurveyMonkey, Zoomerang, SurveyGizmo) provide you with various features related to questionnaire design. But generally, there are restrictions either on question type or on number of questions, unless you pay additional money. These tools do provide question numbers with questions and also give you spreadsheets and visualizations of the data that can help in your analysis process.

You also have the option of distributing your questionnaire in paper form. This may be easier for you, in the sense that you can create the questions in a Word document. Some researchers prefer to work with hard copies of completed questionnaires, which is another reason why distributing them in person may be the right mode for you. In addition, this would allow students to clarify questions that they may have as they are completing the questionnaire, something that is not as easy to do when completing a questionnaire online.

However, if you distribute your questionnaire in class, for example, then this may get into ethical issues (e.g. related to roles and responsibilities) because students may perceive you *teacher or researcher?*

as their teacher asking them to complete a questionnaire. Distributing questionnaires in person can raise some issues, especially if you are giving them to your own students. Since they may be used to seeing you as their instructor within the classroom setting, your handing something out for them to fill out may feel like an exam (as opposed to a research instrument for your research project). Moving the completion of the questionnaire outside of the classroom context itself can mitigate these effects. You could consider gathering them in a space other than your classroom, however, if you choose to distribute the questionnaire to them in person. In-person distribution can ensure that you will get the questionnaires back.

It can be difficult at times for people to respond honestly to a questionnaire when the researcher seems to be 'waiting' for them to finish it. This goes against the 'asynchronous' nature of questionnaires. And there may be a perception that you as the researcher know who they are as respondents (even if the questionnaire itself is anonymous), and this may also cause them to respond less than honestly. However, you could distribute the questionnaire in paper form and then ask for it back at another time (or have them drop it off in a box outside your office). This can help with (though not completely getting rid of) some of the issues involved with this questionnaire distribution method.

You will also want to consider the timing of your data collection. Will you be distributing the questionnaire only once? Will you compare data from different questionnaires distributed over time? These issues are important to consider early on in the process.

Sampling

Now that you have created your questionnaire and piloted it, you can think through in more detail who the population will be. When you distribute a questionnaire, you may be interested in a particular population (called the 'universe' for your research). Generally speaking, however, we must always select a sample of that larger 'universe' from which to collect our data. For example, perhaps for your research project the 'universe' may be all inter-national students from a particular country who take ESL classes at your institution. But, the sample may only come from students in particular classes or taught by certain faculty. The goal is to select a sampling process that does not include bias or a priori selection of particular students. This is an important methodo-logical step, which (if done well) can enhance outsiders' assess-ments of the rigorousness of your research process.

There are six main ways to sample, each of which can be applied to the collection of quantitative data as well (Wagner, 2015, pp. 85–86; also discussed in Balnaves and Caputi, 2001, p. 94):

Random sampling: goal of being "truly representative" of population, "equal chance" of being selected to be in the study

Stratified random sample: "subgroups are selected", and samples are "generated for each subgroup"

Systematic sampling: "every nth person is selected"

Cluster sampling: "natural subgroups (clusters) can be identified", "random samples are generated for each of the clusters"

Convenience sampling: "individuals who are readily available and who the researcher has access to"

Snowball sampling (Balnaves and Caputi, 2001, p. 95): "relies on the researcher's knowledge of the situation and the people he or she knows. The researcher contacts people relevant to him or her"

It is important to be aware of the range of sampling options so that you can make an informed decision based on what will work best for you.

Bias and Possible Errors in Questionnaire Data Collection

Any research method has the potential for bias and error (Wagner, 2015, p. 87). Nonresponse bias can be counteracted by including as many participants as possible, such that if some do not respond, then you still have a useful number of participants. Measurement error is an error based on the participants' having not understood what the questions were asking. One way to counteract this is to provide an example of the kind of response you are looking for. Coverage error is an error based on your not getting as many participants as you could have. One way to counteract this is to make sure that all email addresses are up to date. Sampling error is an error in which the wrong people respond to the questionnaire. If you are distributing the questionnaire in person, then it is less likely that this error would occur.

Research Validity

Three issues that may affect questionnaire data in particular are research construct, fatigue and bias (Wagner, 2015). Research construct is whether you are able to capture data on what you are interested in measuring (e.g. student satisfaction). Fatigue is whether the questionnaire design is causing participants to respond in ways that are not authentic. Bias can also affect responses (e.g, prestige – enhance one's own standing, self-deception – how they would like to think of themselves vs how they really act, acquiescence – imagining what the researcher wants to read). It is important to keep all of these issues in mind when you design your questionnaire so that you can mitigate its effects.

Alone or Together?

One last issue to consider is whether you want to use questionnaire data on its own or in combination with other data collection methods. In many cases questionnaire data can strike a great balance of efficiency and richness. The data is easily comparable, and themes can emerge fairly quickly. Therefore, it may be enough on its own. However, since questionnaires are best at capturing ideologies, it might also be necessary to combine questionnaires with other data collection methods (e.g. interviews, participant-observation). Questionnaires can therefore be a first step in a suite of data collection, meant to primarily capture 'what'. And then interviews can help you go into more depth with fewer participants, to begin exploring 'how' and 'why' in relation to your research question. The main thing to think about when deciding about this 'alone or together' issue is which methods will provide you with the kind of information you need to answer your research question – that is what you should always go back to throughout the research process. In addition, you may consider giving participants a questionnaire at a certain point in time and then giving them the same (or a different) questionnaire later in time so that you can compare and contrast the results. This is quite common for longitudinal studies and those in which an 'intervention' occurred after which you seek to measure a change in the participants.

Questionnaire Data Analysis

Questionnaires can involve multiple data analysis steps since they may include multiple types of question. You may analyse your qualitative data by using interpretive analytical methods, including coding and content analysis. You may analyse quantitative questions by using descriptive statistics, measures of reliability and factor analysis. These various options for data analysis will be discussed in further detail in Chapters 10 and 11.

Suggested Readings

http://psr.iq.harvard.edu/book/questionnaire-design-tip-sheet
    This useful resource provides readers with key issues to consider when designing effective questionnaires, specifically focused on

the wording of questions as well as question types. It also includes a helpful list of what to include and what to avoid when designing questionnaires. There are additional resources provided as well.

http://www.socialresearchmethods.net/kb/questype.php
This resource gives an overview of basic question types for questionnaires, especially useful for those researchers who are just learning how to create and design questionnaires.

https://zapier.com/learn/ultimate-guide-to-forms-and-surveys/best-survey-apps/
This resource can help you decide which online mode of distributing your questionnaire may be most useful for your purposes.

CHAPTER 6

Interviews, Focus Groups and Reflections

Guiding Questions:

1. Have you ever been interviewed? What was the experience like?
2. Do you think that interviews are an effective way to learn about someone's views and actions? How about focus groups? Why? Why not?
3. What are some things you think about in relation to your teaching, virtually every day? Do you ever share those thoughts with anyone else? If so, in what formats (phone call, text, Skype, email, in person)?
4. Do you use structured reflection in your own professional practice? Why? Why not?
5. Do you encourage your students to use structured reflection? Why? Why not?

Introduction

In this chapter, we will discuss the range of options for collecting interview data (Ho, 2012; Talmy and Richards, 2011; Richards, 2009), on its own and in combination with other data collection methods. The chapter will provide an overview of open-ended (unstructured/informal), semi-structured and structured (standardized) interview methods (see Merriam, 2009, p. 89 for a helpful table with defining features of each). There will also be hands-on activities designed to allow you the opportunity to practise a variety of interview techniques. Focus groups as a potential methodology will also be touched upon. In addition, we will discuss the use of various types of reflection, using Murphy's (2014) discussion of reflection-in-action (present), reflection-on-action (past) and reflection-for-action (future) that builds upon Schön's (1984, 1987) research on reflective practitioners. We will focus on how teachers themselves can create and analyse individual reflection journals and collaborative reflections to think through their own practice (cf. Wallace, 1991; Hanson, 2008; Husu et al., 2008). Reflexivity is an important aspect of reflection. Reflexivity is 'in part, critically thinking about how one's status characteristics, values, and history, as well as the numerous choices one has made during the research, affect the results' (Bailey, 2007, p. 6). In addition, you will learn about tools and reflection prompts for students, which can then be analysed using discourse and content analytic methods. There will be some treatment of think-aloud activities and stimulated recall protocols as modes of reflection. The chapter will also provide samples of teachers' reflection journals and students' reflections (e.g. on a learning management system like Moodle).

Why Interview?

In the previous chapter, we discussed the use of questionnaires, which are one type of survey. Survey research is intended to 'generalize from a sample to a population' (Fowler, 2009, as cited in Creswell, 2014, p. 13). The other type of survey is interviews, a well-known research methodology that can provide a great deal of depth about particular topics. As Patton (2002, pp. 340–341) notes,

> We interview people to find out from them those things we cannot directly observe. … We cannot observe feelings, thoughts, and intentions. We cannot observe behaviours that took place at

some previous point in time. We cannot observe situations that preclude the presence of an observer. We cannot observe how people have organized the world and the meanings they attach to what goes on in the world. We have to ask people questions about those things. The purpose of interviewing, then, is to allow us to enter into the other person's perspective. The purpose of interviewing, then, is to allow us to enter into the other person's perspective.

Interviews can allow you as the researcher to explore the full range of the *what, how and why* of an individual's experience. One does need time, energy and effort in order to interview research participants (especially groups of people). However, the benefits can be great since interview responses can shed light and depth on a range of topics that may interest you as a researcher. When selecting an appropriate interview methodology, you can select from the three (broad) categories: person-centred/open-ended, semi-structured and structured, depending upon your purposes.

Interviews are similar to questionnaires in some ways (see Bernard, 2011 for further discussion). Structured interviews are perhaps closest to questionnaires since they have a set list of questions that every respondent is asked. Structured interviews are a face-to-face equivalent of questionnaires. We may in fact use questionnaires in a face-to-face interview. One issue to consider when conducting interviews is location. It is important to select a location for the interview that increases the interviewee's comfort and anonymity. Therefore, conducting an interview in your own classroom may not be the best idea even if it may be easy or efficient. It is important to ask the interviewee where they would feel most comfortable.

Interviews are different from questionnaires in that they are synchronous and have the ability to be more open-ended, allowing for more back-and-forth, clarification and elaboration than questionnaires. They are therefore especially well-suited as a data collection technique about language learners. For example, I frequently highlight for my teaching English as a second language/teaching foreign language (TESOL/TFL) students the importance of collecting their students' language learner histories early in the semester so that they will have an in-depth understanding of students' backgrounds, interests and experiences. Though potentially time intensive, interviews can provide a wealth of information that can inform your professional practice (cf. Coffey and Street, 2008; Talmy, 2011; Talmy and Richards, 2011). (See more about language learner histories in the description of VIVID pictures, described in Chapter 7). You might also be interested in interviewing other teachers at your teaching site to provide yourself with narratives (Pavlenko, 2007) that are relevant to your research questions. It is important that before beginning your interview, you explain to your interviewees the purpose of your research and why they were selected (similar to the questionnaire description discussed in Chapter 5).

The Interactional Nature of Interviews

As mentioned previously, interviews are synchronous, which means that you are able to respond immediately to your interviewees. This may make some interviews feel more like conversations. This back-and-forth can come in the form of minimal responses (e.g. mmhmm, uh huh), the clarifications/paraphrasing that you do, and the questions and follow-up questions that you ask. Therefore, even if you have a 'script' for your interview, no two interviews are alike. This is part of what can make them so interesting to do and to analyse. By their very nature, interviews are emergent and cannot be planned (Briggs, 1986, 2007; Koven, 2014). It also means that it will be necessary for you to develop skills over time in how you respond to your interviewees' responses, remaining neutral while engaged and interested. It is impossible for your responses to not have an effect on the interviewee, but the effects can be mitigated if you practise interviewing before engaging in the research interviews themselves. Just as you would pilot a questionnaire, you can pilot an interview – to practise these necessary skills.

The interactional nature of interviews also means that your interviewees are tracking how they are perceived while they are responding. They may also shape their responses based on their relationship with you and how they believe the responses may be used. This is another reason why it is important to practise interviewing: so that you can have as much useable data as possible, which you can compare and contrast most easily. It is important to tolerate silence and respect the interviewee's agenda (in addition to being aware of your own). Also consider if you will interview the person side by side or face to face, depending on their and your comfort level and goals. In addition, you can consider whether to record, take notes, or not to make records at all during the interview. It is also relevant to decide which language(s) you will use to conduct the interview, based on your research goals, relationship to the interviewee and language proficiencies.

ACTIVITY 6.1

What might be some pros and cons for recording or not recording interviews for your research project? What do you plan to do? Why?

Structured Interviews

Structured interviews are closest to questionnaires in that you prepare set questions in advance, which are designed in a thoughtful way to elicit information relevant to your research question. There may be less back-and-forth in structured interviews than in other, less-structured types because your intention is to get through the same set of questions with all of your interviewees. The information you learn through structured interviews can be more easily comparable across respondents and questions because of how they are designed. However, they do not always allow interviewees to explore in detail the full range of issues associated with particular questions. Structured interviews should include a number of open-ended questions, in order to take advantage of the more fluid nature (different from asynchronous surveys). Similar issues raised in the previous chapter in relation to question design apply to structured interviews as well. However, there is some opportunity to negotiate meaning since one of the affordances of interviews is that they are synchronous. This is of course especially useful when interviewing language learners.

Structured interviews, like questionnaires, should be organized in order to make the interviewees comfortable early on. As mentioned in relation to questionnaires, once you have built rapport, you can delve into more 'objectionable' topics. Since in many cases you may be interviewing your own students you also need to keep in mind issues of bias (in terms of what they may or may not be willing to respond to, especially with you sitting right there).

Example Interview Protocol for a (Short) Structured Interview

Inductive Research Question

What are the experiences of Chinese heritage learners in a high school Chinese class?

1. Where did you grow up?
2. Where did you learn Chinese? Whom did you/do you use Chinese with?
3. What do you like about learning language in your Chinese class? Why?
4. What do you not like about learning language in your Chinese class? Why?
5. What do you find easy in your Chinese class? Why?
6. What do you find difficult in your Chinese class? Why?
7. Is there something you'd like to add? Please share.

ACTIVITY 6.2

What is one research purpose you have in mind for which a set of structured interviews would be most suited? Why?

Semi-Structured Interviews

Semi-structured interviews (Bailey 2007, p. 100) start with a set of topics (and perhaps an interview/question guide) but allow for more fluidity and back-and-forth to emerge over the course of the interview. The interview guide 'will probably contain several specific questions that you want to ask everyone, some more open-ended questions that could be followed up with probes, and perhaps a list of some areas, topics and issues that you want to know more about but do not have enough information about at the outset of your study to form specific questions' (Merriam, 2009, p. 103). They have the potential to involve more pattern-seeking during the analysis phase, but not quite as much as open-ended interviews. For a research study you may be interested in interviewing your principal. If you would like to explore his/her educational philosophy, a **semi-structured interview** may be fitting since it not only allows for some structure but also allows for some exploration through the investigation of various prompts in the interview process itself.

ACTIVITY 6.3

1. Is there someone in your teaching context whom you would like to interview?
2. What topics and one or two questions are you interested in exploring with this person?

ACTIVITY 6.4

Select a topic of interest to you and create five to ten interview questions that relate to it. Practise using a semi-structured interview format with a colleague. Practise both interviewing and being interviewed. What was the experience like in each case?

Open-Ended/Person-Centred Interviews

Open-ended interviews can allow you to learn about an interviewee without setting a particular agenda in advance. If you are interested in learning about your students' language learning histories as a way to explore what might be most useful to them as learners, then open-ended interviews may be the right choice for you. This inductive approach would allow themes and patterns to emerge without your having a set agenda in advance. An example of a first question in a **person-centred interview** (Hollan, 2001; Levy and Hollan, 1998) might be 'tell me about your life' or 'tell me about your experience learning languages'. Once the person starts sharing on this broad topic, you can ask questions as they become relevant. This involves actively listening and not leading the interviewee based on your primary interests. These interviews can be very rich since they allow the interviewee to determine in large part the direction, content and depth of the interview. Person-centred interviews can be even more effective when they are done multiple times with the same people, as this allows for meanings to be negotiated over time. In these cases, your interviewee may touch upon the same topics in different interview contexts, which allows for more depth and layers in your analysis. Interviews can also be combined with ethnographic observations, suc' you can better understand your observations and as' patterns.

Effective Interviewing

As mentioned previously, it is important to remain objective but engaged while interviewing someone. Below are useful guidelines in this regard from Genzuk, 2003 (quoted exactly from https://education.ucf.edu/mirc/docs/pp/FlaRE%20Profes sional%20Paper%20-%20Ethnographic%20Research.pdf):

1. Ask open-ended, clear questions using understandable and appropriate language.
2. Use probes and follow-up questions to solicit depth and detail.
3. Listen attentively and respond appropriately to let the person know he or she is being heard.[1]
4. Observe while interviewing.
5. Be aware of and sensitive to how the person is affected and responds to different questions.
6. Tape record whenever possible to capture full and exact quotations for analysis and reporting.

The Importance of Listening

No matter which type of interview you select, the importance of effective listening cannot be overstated. Listening is the heart of great interviews. It is important that interviewees be understood on their own terms, without their sensing a bias to respond in a particular way. This means that you would need to be sensitive to even small things like when and how much you use minimal responses (e.g. mmhmm, uh huh), as these can make the interviewee believe you think some things are interesting while others are not. This may implicitly make them continue telling certain stories while cutting others short. In addition, all interviews are defined by the fact that interviewees' relationships with you as the researcher and their perceptions of you and

---

1 Here you can use 'interpretive questions', which allow the 'investigator to confirm the tentative interpretation of what [has] been said in the interview' (Merriam, 2009, p. 99).

your research interests shape their responses. There is no way to get around this, but it is important to be aware of this when designing interviews and engaging in them.

Interviewing Tools

Interviews are generally conducted face to face, especially in situations when you are doing research on a classroom for which you serve as the teacher. Tools like Skype, Google Hangout and Adobe Connect can also be very useful for interviews (especially for online courses). In many cases these tools can also allow you to record the interviews (audio and/or video), which provides you with the necessary material to go back and analyse your data.

Focus Groups

Questionnaires and interviews allow you to understand the perspectives of one individual at a time, and as the analyst, you then compare and contrast across individuals. A focus group, 'recruited to discuss a particular topic' (Bernard, 2011, p. 172), is 'a small group of six to ten people led through an open discussion by a skilled moderator. The group needs to be large enough to generate rich discussion but not so large that some participants are left out' (Eliot & Associates, 2005, p. 1). They are synchronous (usually semi-structured) interviews of more than one person, who are part of a sample you are interested in for your research question.

Focus groups can allow participants to learn from one another and share in ways that they otherwise may not have, by using other data collection methods, which can provide you with very rich data (cf. Kruger and Casey, 2008). Participants can be influenced by one another (based on relationships outside the research context and on what is happening in the local interaction), which means that their responses may or may not reflect what they might have shared on their own. However, focus groups are unique since they can provide you with rich data that may complement what you are collecting through other research methods, to help you 'gather preliminary data, aid in the development of surveys and interview guides, and clarify research findings from another method' (Cohen and Crabtree, 2006). For example, if focus groups are used to complement other data collection methods, then these seeming 'mismatches' can be fruitful information for data analysis.

There are a number of reasons that you might choose to collect focus group data, on its own or in conjunction with other data collection methods. As noted by Cohen and Crabtree (2006), focus groups allow researchers

1. to explore new research areas
2. to explore a topic that is difficult to observe or does not lend itself to observational techniques
3. to explore sensitive topics
4. to collect a concentrated set of observations in a short time span
5. to ascertain perspectives and experiences from people on a topic (e.g. those who might otherwise be marginalized)

Focus groups involve a great deal of effective facilitation, which is related to the ideas about active listening above. In many ways, a well-led focus group is like an effective language lesson, since it involves coordination and negotiation among multiple parties to make sure that everyone's voice is heard. Moderating a focus group 'requires the combined skills of an ethnographer, a survey researcher, and a therapist' (Bernard, 2011, p. 175). Below are some guidelines for an effective focus group facilitator (Eliott & Associates, 2005):

1. can listen attentively with sensitivity and empathy
2. is able to listen and think at the same time
3. believes that all group participants have something to offer no matter what their education, experience, or background
4. has adequate knowledge of the topic

5. can keep personal views and ego out of the facilitation
6. is someone the group can relate to but also give authority to
7. can appropriately manage challenging group dynamics

Generally speaking, it is good practice to (audio or video) record focus groups (Bernard, 2011, p. 176), as this will facilitate the process of transcription and eventual analysis. Another option would be for someone other than the facilitator to take notes, but these can capture only so much – especially since there are so many participants in a focus group and therefore a great deal to keep track of. Once you are analysing data from the focus groups, it is important to keep in mind a range of effects that may have influenced participants' interactions and responses: response effects, deference effect, social desirability effect and the-third-party-present effect (Bernard, 2011, pp. 176–181). In addition, some questions may be perceived as threatening or nonthreatening (Bernard, 2011, p. 181); therefore, it is important that your focus group guide/prompts are well constructed. In addition, you will need to develop your abilities to create culturally sensitive questions on the spot, something you can perhaps practise with a few colleagues in advance of conducting the focus group.

ACTIVITY 6.5

What is a topic you would like to explore through a focus group? Who would be included in the focus group? What are some questions you could ask during the focus group?

Production Tasks

Production tasks are 'techniques used to obtain samples of learner language, typically in order to study processes and stages of development that learners pass through as they develop their second language proficiency' (Nunan and Bailey, 2009, p. 321). They can be used in combination with interviews, in order to collect data for both language and content analysis (Nunan, personal communication). Some examples are discourse completion tasks (setting up a situation and then eliciting responses from learners), role plays (imagining situations and then eliciting responses from learners), tests and picture description tasks (for further description of these methods, see Nunan and Bailey, 2009, pp. 321–328). Though not naturalistic by nature, production tasks can provide useful information for researchers interested in their learners' language but perhaps lacking the time or resources for extended periods of naturalistic observation (Nunan and Bailey, 2009, p. 321) and can include investigations of negotiation of meaning as well as learner proficiency.

What is Structured Reflection? Why Do it?

Engaging in inquiry is a reflective process. **Reflection** is sense-making about actions, the metacognitive work that one engages in to process an activity before, during and/or after it happens. Building upon Schön's (1984, 1987) research on reflective practitioners, Murphy (2014) provides a useful typology that includes reflection-in-action (present), reflection-on-action (past) and reflection-for-action (future). Reflection is important for language teachers (cf. Farrell, 2007), who are continuously thinking through and improving their own professional practice, and for students, who can be challenged to make sense of their own language learning and experiences.

When engaging in reflection, three components are essential: open-mindedness, responsibility and wholeheartedness (Dewey, 1993; Zeichner and Liston, 1996). Not only is it important that teachers and students engage in reflection, but it is important that reflection be structured. Structure allows for some comparison across reflections, and it therefore provides a chance for themes and patterns to emerge over time. For example, keeping a regular journal with one's thoughts can provide interesting depth for your research.

A useful distinction is that between reflection and Reflection. The unplanned reflections that we do every day can be referred to as 'small r' reflection. 'Everyday, unplanned reflection' is 'small r' reflection (Wilmes, personal communication, as cited in O'Grady, 2000). More 'intentionally designed Reflection activities' are called 'capital R' reflection (Wilmes, personal communication, as cited in O'Grady, 2000) (e.g. structured journals, the 'what', 'so what', 'now what' typology). One way to think about this is that the ongoing reflection that we do every day (on our way home, in the shower) might be called 'formative reflection', whereas the more intentional and planned reflection might be called 'summative reflection'. Through the development of a **Reflection Repertoire**, we ask and answer these fundamental questions:

What do I do? How do I do it? What does this mean for both myself as a professional and those whom I serve? (http://oregonstate.edu/instruct/pte/module2/rp.htm)

ACTIVITY 6.6

Think about a typical day during the week. When do you usually reflect on your teaching? During your morning drive? During your lunch break? After dinner? How can you make any of those reflection times more structured? What can you realistically add to your reflection repertoire each day?

ACTIVITY 6.7

Do you currently use reflection-in-action, reflection-on-action and/ or reflection-for-action? Is there one that you engage in more often than the others? Why? Is there one you would like to try to do more often? Why? How might you start? What are some ways that you could use structured reflection that you have not yet used so far?

Selecting a Reflection Approach that Works for You

As a teacher-researcher it is essential to create a reflection repertoire that you can reasonably stick to. The main thing to consider is what your goals are in engaging in a particular reflection practice: Do you want to process how a particular class went? Do you want to think through effective options for this particular class? For other classes you might teach in the future? To create a research question you would like to explore in this and future classes?

There are a number of reflection options you can choose from, all of which have their positives and negatives. You can create *individual* reflection journals that allow you to think in depth about your pedagogical approaches and choices. You may or may not share those with someone else. You can reflect in *collaborative* ways, in person or online. Below are some reflection typologies that may be useful for you:

- Experiencing – Sharing – Processing – Generalizing – Applying
  This is connected with Kolb's (1994) **experiential learning** cycle.
- Continuous – Connected – Challenging – Contextualized
  http://www.fresnostate.edu/academics/cesl/facultysl/five/value.html
- Pre-Reflection (or Preflection), During-Reflection, Post-Reflection
  This connects with Murphy's typology, in that allows for the range of possibilities for when and how to reflect.
- What – So What – Now What
  This provides you with an opportunity to think through and describe what happened, determine why it is important to you/raised relevant issues and figure out next steps/what it means for the future.
  http://www.servicelearning.umn.edu/info/reflection.html
- DEAL: Describe (experience objectively, assess progress since last reflection) Examine (personal, communal, academic perspectives), Articulate Learning (what, how, why)
  This typology comes from service-learning and connects reflection to current academic learning. This is especially useful for students and student teachers.

http://servicelearning.duke.edu/uploads/media_items/deal-reflection-questions.original.pdf
- **Critical Incidents** (describe in detail something unexpected, critically analyse how you handled it, consider what you might do in future situations, what this means about you as a language teacher) (cf. Tripp, 2012; Nunan and Choi, 2010; Critical events in Bailey, 2007)

This allows teachers to think through what they expect and what they did not expect, as well as how they handled a situation. Like other reflection tools, it provides an opportunity for discussion of possible future applications.

All of these reflection tools can be used for your research, in terms of your own reflections, your colleagues' reflections and your students' reflections. And the products can be analysed using discourse and content analytic methods (to be discussed in further detail in Chapter 10).

ACTIVITY 6.8

Select one of the reflection typologies above, and use it to explore your perspectives on a particular lesson that relates to your research question. Did you find the reflection process to be useful? Why? Why not?

Teacher Journals and Diaries

A teacher journal or a teacher diary is another useful tool for engaging in reflective practice, which can be analysed for your research studies. These may be in addition to verbal commentaries and self-report instruments (Borg, 2009). Diary studies have been pervasive in the language education research field (cf., Bailey, 1991). They are a form of case study research that can help to illuminate patterns in a teacher's thought processes over time.

ACTIVITY 6.9

Select a teaching event, and use the following format[2] as a guide for your reflection journal:

Heading: date, location, time, class/event involved, topic or issues involved (if appropriate)

Background: describe the class/event – participants, nature of course content and activities, general goals, specific objectives related to this journal

Narrative: describe what happened, including only the information relevant to the focal issue (fully detailed accounts are not necessary)

Reflection: discuss what you learned from your reflections on the events described, what this means for your teaching and/or your understanding of teaching/learning processes, what you are planning in light of this learning in terms of your own teaching, how you now interpret relevant theory and research

Tools for Student Reflection

Many of the tools/formats/typologies listed above could reasonably be used by students in structured reflection. In addition to tools for teacher reflection, there are established research methods in applied linguistics that incorporate reflection in some way. For example, stimulated recall methods (cf. Gass and Mackey, 2017) integrate metacognitive awareness and abilities with assessment. Introspective tasks like think-aloud procedures, 'where participants voice their thoughts while completing a task' (Rose, 2015, p. 427), are very useful for a variety of research purposes (Gu, 2014; Hyland, 2010).

---

2 Guidelines influenced by Zeichner and Liston's (1996) *Reflective Teaching: An Introduction*

In particular, they are frequently used to research reading (Stevenson, 2015) and writing. Retrospective interviews allow the learners to describe after the fact their procedure for completing particular tasks – unlike think-aloud procedures, which are done while the task is being completed. These interviews can reduce the cognitive load for learners and may be more appropriate for younger learners with less experience with voicing of metacognitive strategies. You could ask students to write diaries or journals to document their learning process and experience and then analyse those using discourse and content analysis.

All of these reflection-oriented activities can provide you with rich data about your students' metacognitive perspectives. Students can keep their own reflective journals, in which they analyse the what and the how of their experiences.

Cultural Aspects of Reflection

It is important to keep in mind that reflection is a culturally bound activity. For example, students from different cultural and linguistic backgrounds may feel more or less comfortable sharing their reflections in a public forum. Therefore, it is important to allow for a range of reflection types and formats so that students can both feel comfortable and be challenged to go outside their comfort zone. This also relates to research ethics. If the students know, for example, that their reflections (even in anonymized form) may be shared at a conference or in a publication (beyond their own class), they may be more or less inclined to be honest about their experience. These issues relate to politeness (Brown and Levinson, 1987), respect and power dynamics. Students may perceive that if they say 'yes' to being involved in your research, then they may be more polite and demonstrate respect towards you because they see you in a more powerful position. It is important for us as researchers to be aware of these power dynamics in our research design and to conduct ourselves ethically in all research encounters.

Conclusion

Interviews, focus groups and reflections provide you with a multitude of methods for gathering rich information about your and your students' ideologies and practices. These are all flexible methods that can be shaped in the ways that are most useful to you.

Suggested Readings

http://designresearchtechniques.com/casestudies/semi-structured-interviews/

This short online resource provides key concepts and guiding questions for conducting semi-structured interviews, synthesized from key literature on research methods.

http://www.jhsph.edu/research/centers-and-institutes/center-for-refugee-and-disaster-response/publications_tools/publications/_pdf/pr_apx-b_ethnographic.PDF

This useful online resource highlights effective ethnographic interviewing techniques, along with sample interview transcripts that include key concepts.

http://www.qualres.org/index.html

This comprehensive online resource provides readers with basic concepts for a range of research methods, including interviews and focus groups.

7 Case Studies, Ethnography and Visual Data

Guiding Questions:

1. What are some cultures you consider yourself to be a part of? What makes you a member of those cultures?
2. In what ways do classrooms constitute cultures?
3. Do you enjoy observing people? Why? Why not? Do you enjoy being observed? Why? Why not?
4. Do you ever find yourself observing your students in your language classroom? When? Why? How?
5. Do you believe that the patterns and interactions you see in your classroom are similar to or different from other classrooms? Why?
6. Do you consider yourself a visual learner? A visual teacher? Why?
7. Do you have experience with video- or audio-recording?
8. Do you enjoy taking photographs?
9. How might you use (audio or video) recordings as a research methodology?
10. What are some visual ways that you could approach your research?

Introduction

This chapter will focus on case studies, ethnography (cf., LeCompte and Schensul, 2010; Shaw, 1996; Watson-Gegeo, 1988) and visual data collection, as means to capture and analyse practices (what individuals, groups and communities do on a daily basis). As you continue reading and working through the activities in these chapters, you can begin to consider how these various methods may complement one another for the purpose of answering a particular research question. In this chapter, you will have the opportunity to learn about ethnographic methods, including participant-observation and **field notes**. This chapter will include examples of language classroom data stemming from ethnographic studies. It will also discuss case studies in some detail, as well as various visual approaches (e.g, photographs, maps and tracking). There will also be some discussion of issues related to video and audio-recordings, including frame grabs and subtitles.

What is Culture?

One of the fundamental assumptions underpinning an ethnographic approach to research in language teaching is the idea that classrooms are cultures. What constitutes a culture? Who counts as a member of a culture? One source highlights seven key components to consider when describing cultures: symbols, beliefs, values, norms, religion, rewards and punishments and artefacts (Harrison, 2011). Are there any components in this list that are not relevant to classroom cultures? Are there any other components that you might add to this list? For decades, researchers have highlighted the fact that cultures and speech communities are based upon shared norms (for an overview, see Avineri and Kroskrity, 2014). However, more recent research highlights the diversity within communities of practice (Eckert and McConnell-Ginet, 1992; Lave and Wenger, 1991; Wenger, 2000). In Kaplan-Weinger and Ullman's (2015) discussion of classroom cultures, they highlight the following key components of culture (pp. 3–4):

1. Culture is not bounded for most people who live in urban areas.
2. Cultural groups vary a lot.
3. Cultures are constantly changing.
4. Cultural knowledge is often below our consciousness.
5. Cultural knowledge impacts how we interpret the world around us.
6. Culture is in our everyday practices.
7. Culture(s) give us certain positions and biases.

These more recent conceptualizations of culture and community are useful in providing a framework for thinking about classrooms as cultures.

Classrooms as Cultures

There are numerous ways that we can consider the classrooms in which we teach and learn to be considered cultures. Students and teachers constantly engage in language socialization practices (Ochs and Schieffelin, 1984; Schieffelin and Ochs, 1986), in which linguistic and cultural learning are intertwined. Students and teachers negotiate norms and beliefs as they relate to classroom interactions. Interactions are shaped by the beliefs and experiences that individuals bring to the classroom context. Ethnographic methods can provide useful lenses to capture the shifting nature of interactions and practices in classrooms, since students and teachers are constantly negotiating interactions in relation to one another. We can also consider the institutions where we work to be cultures, with subcultures within them (task culture, role culture, etc.).

Case Studies

Case studies are a well-known research methodology in applied linguistics (Duff, 2008, 2014; Richards, 1998), focused on an in-depth examination of an individual, person, context, or situation. The case study, though a 'single bounded unit' (Duff, 2013), is selected because it includes aspects that are potentially generalizable. In language education, case studies are frequently focused on an individual student, an individual teacher, or an individual classroom. They involve 'rich contextualization and a deep, inductive analysis of data from a small set of participants, sites, or events in order to understand aspects of language learning or use' (Duff, 2013). They provide 'concrete instances of a phenomenon of interest' (Duff, 2013). Conducting an ethnography in your own classroom would be an example of a case study, with the single bounded unit being your classroom. Observing, interviewing, collecting linguistic data from and collecting a participant diary from one of the learners in your classroom would be another example of a case study, with the single bounded unit being the student. Case studies can be effective since they allow the researcher to consider one unit in depth, therefore understanding its component parts in detail.

ACTIVITY 7.1

Is there a learner in your classroom whose experience or linguistic proficiency you would like to examine in depth? What data might you collect? Do you think this would be fairly easy or difficult to undertake? Why?

Why Ethnography?

Ethnography is 'the written description of the social organization, social activities, symbolic and material resources and interpretive practices characteristic of a particular group of people' (Duranti, 1997, p. 85). Ethnography is a common interpretive method in a number of social sciences, including anthropology and sociology. It is intended to provide a longitudinal (long-term), in-depth understanding of the beliefs and practices of a group of people. This ecological view can capture changes over time, for example the ways that identities may shift. Ethnographic methods that can capture practices (e.g. observations, field notes) can be used in combination with ethnographic methods that are best suited to capture ideologies and reports of behaviour (e.g. questionnaires, focus groups). Below we will highlight a number of key concepts that are relevant to a discussion of ethnographic methods: familiar/strange, emic/**etic**, cultural relativism/ethnocentrism and positionality.

Familiar/Strange

When a researcher engages in ethnography they are seeking to make that which is familiar into something strange and that which is strange into something familiar (Kaplan-Weinger and Ullman, 2015). When making something familiar strange, this means that we examine in-depth practices that we might otherwise take for granted, in order to understand them from an outsider's point of view. For example, in many American households we keep our shoes on when entering someone else's home as a guest, whereas in many Japanese households the expectation is that we should take our shoes off. If I am used to keeping my shoes on, I need to ask myself questions about why that is, what the alternatives are and what the beliefs that might underpin this practice are. And if I go to a Japanese household and am asked to take off my shoes (which may seem strange at first), I need to examine this practice in a way that makes it familiar (trying to understand the beliefs that underpin it, from an insider's perspective). An ethnographer's main goal is to constantly inquire about the *hows* and *whys* behind the *whats* that we see in particular cultures, doing our best to remain as objective and curious as possible. This means that we hold off on interpreting what we see before we sufficiently understand the cultural or linguistic practice on its own terms.

ACTIVITY 7.2

Identify a cultural practice you have observed but know relatively little about. How can you find out more about that cultural practice, in order to make the strange familiar? What are some questions you might ask someone who engages regularly in that cultural practice? Now identify a cultural practice you engage in (e.g. ordering coffee at a local coffee shop) and think about all the ways you could make that familiar cultural practice strange. How would you explain that practice to someone who has never seen or heard of it before?

Emic/Etic

The notion of familiar/strange is closely connected to another key component of ethnography, focused on emic and etic perspectives (Duranti, 1997). 'Emic' means an insider's view and 'etic' means an outsider's view. When observing, analysing and interpreting a culture, our goal is to understand practices from the perspective of those who are part of the culture. This means taking on the perspective of someone else and at its core involves empathy. At first it is easy to ask questions and be curious about what may seem strange. That is fine, as long as unnecessary judgement and evaluation go along with it. However, over time the idea is that we are understanding that culture on its own terms, not in relation to our own expectations about how things are 'supposed' to work. This mindset/disposition can free us from our own biases, allowing us to understand human beings and their practices in different ways.

Ethnocentrism vs Cultural Relativism

One component of taking on an 'emic' perspective involves objectivity (vs subjectivity). This means that you are doing your best to look at cultures without judgement or evaluation. Cultural relativism means that you are considering each culture on its own terms, as opposed to believing that the cultures that you are a part of or are familiar with are correct or better. It can be difficult at first to move away from an ethnocentric mindset in which your particular practices are seen as right, but over time you can learn skills and strategies for developing a mindset that moves away from judgement and moves towards deeper understanding of human beings and cultures.

ACTIVITY 7.3

This activity is best done in pairs and it can help you to distinguish between objective description and subjective interpretation. Use the framework provided here: https://dschool.stanford.edu/wp-content/themes/dschool/method-cards/what-why-how.pdf

Ask someone you know to share with you a picture of something they have experienced (on vacation, at school, with family, etc.). Use the what-how-why method to describe and interpret what you believe is happening in the picture. What = objective description (especially nouns and verbs). How = additional layers of description (adjectives and adverbs). Why = interpretation. Make sure to spend at least five minutes on each component of the framework, to begin training yourself in objective description before interpretation. If possible, share with the other person your what-how-why and find out from them their what-how-why of that picture. It is also useful if they can do the same for you, based on a picture of an experience that you have had.

Was this activity easy? Difficult? Why? How might you further develop these skills of description vs interpretation?

Positionality

Ethnography is at its core one human being's interpretation of the practices and behaviours of other human beings. This involves a great deal of subjectivity, meaning that the data collection and analysis is always coming from a particular set of perspectives. Another key component of ethnography, therefore, is an acknowledgement of one's positionality, meaning that you recognize how your own perspectives and identities may have an impact on your findings and conclusions (see the Appendix at the end of this chapter for an example of a positionality statement). Though our goal in ethnography may be objective description and analysis, we must acknowledge our own subjectivities. This is especially true in action research since we have multiple roles (e.g. teacher, researcher, assessor) at any given time in the research process (discussed in relation to ethics in Chapter 4).

REFLECTION 7.1

Which of your identities might shape your approach to your research? Why? In what ways?

Autoethnography

Autoethnography is 'an approach to research and writing that seeks to describe and systematically analyse personal experience in order to understand cultural experience. This approach challenges canonical ways of doing research and representing others and treats research as a political, socially just and socially conscious act. A researcher uses tenets of autobiography and ethnography to do and write autoethnography. Thus, as a method, autoethnography is both process and product' (http://www.qualitative-research.net/index.php/fqs/article/view/1589/3095). Autoethnography is a method that is becoming increasingly popular within applied linguistics. For a great example, read Choi (2016).

Participant-Observation

Participant-observation is one fundamental method that is part of ethnography (Bernard, 2011). We can think of participant-observation as a spectrum along which you may move as a researcher. In some cases, you may be purely observing a classroom, meaning that you are passive or silent. In other cases, you may be participating in the lessons that you are interested in researching. Either way, you are encouraged to 'take a step back' to notice interactions and patterns from the standpoint of an objective researcher. In some inductive research frameworks this part of the process is called 'open noticing', meaning that you are open to seeing things that you were not expecting. This allows you to pursue areas of interest that you may or may not have been planning on.

Observational studies are a well-known research methodology in applied linguistics, as they allow for in-depth analysis of language learners' practices in diverse classrooms. Observations can be structured or unstructured (O'Leary, 2014; Bailey, 2007; for an example of a structured observation guide, see Figure 6.1 in Bailey, 2007, p. 83). Observations can be direct ('watching people and recording their behaviour on the spot' (Bernard, 2011, p. 306) or indirect ('the archeology of human behaviour' (Bernard, 2011, p. 306). Nine features that can be observed (Spradley, 1980) are spaces, objects, actors, acts, activities, events, time, goals and feelings (Bailey, 2007, p. 84).

It is important to keep in mind that observation as a method involves particular issues of subjectivity, bias and ethics. For example, there may be some bias involved in deciding which students we focus on in our observation. And if we are observing in our classrooms, we need to recognize which roles we are in when engaging in an observation from the perspective of a researcher (as opposed to from the perspective of a teacher).

In addition, we need to ensure that we are ethical in what we choose to document and what is 'off limits'. Martinez (2016) highlights some of the complex issues involved in engaging in participant-observation and ethnography in a high school English class where he was a teacher. One interesting method to consider is having multiple people observe in the same context, to move towards reliability and away from subjectivity. The observers can then meet to discuss their observations to ensure sufficient objectivity during the research process. This can be seen, for example, in Greninger's (forthcoming) action research in a Hebrew educational setting. In this case, parents were trained to observe students in different classrooms of different grade levels, as one way to ensure multiple perspectives on the issues at hand. This may not always be possible given the particular constraints of your institution, but you could consider the possibility of multiple observations (e.g. different teachers observing one another's classrooms).

An additional issue to be aware of in relation to observations as a research methodology in classrooms is the pervasiveness of classroom observations conducted for other purposes (e.g. evaluation, ongoing feedback, accreditation, promotion) (O'Leary, 2014). Students may have grown accustomed to having observers in their classrooms who are there primarily to observe their teachers. But it is important that if students are part of what is being observed, then that is made clear to all the participants involved. This highlights the importance of empathy and perspective-taking when engaging in research design that is sensitive to multiple participants.

ACTIVITY 7.4

Have students engage in a learning activity in your own classroom and practise observing in detail what is happening during the activity (noticing who, what, where, when, why and how). Was it easy or difficult to observe objectively (i.e. without evaluation or judgement)? Why? Why not?

Field Notes

As discussed above, ethnography is in depth and longitudinal. It is essential that you engage in detailed record-keeping of the patterns you are observing so that you can track patterns over time. One way to do this is to create field notes. Field notes are a detailed record of your observations that you can refer back to during any phase of your research process. Field notes can include the following information: detailed descriptions, things previously forgotten, analytic ideas and inferences, personal feelings, things to think about and do and reflexive thoughts) (Bailey, 2007, pp. 115–120).

At first your field notes may be quite unstructured, looking more like chronological brainstorming. Over time you will develop notetaking methods that fit your particular interests and purposes. One way to start is to divide up a piece of paper into 'Notetaking' (description of data) and 'Notemaking' (comments and interpretation). In the 'Notetaking' column, you write down only 'what' you see, in as much detail as possible. In the 'Notemaking' column (completed while you're observing and/or afterwards) you make sense of what you wrote, interpreting it and making connections/synthesizing across interactions. Another option would be to divide up the paper into who, what, where, when, why and how. Then over time you might concentrate your notetaking on particular aspects of this typology, once your research focus narrows. You can also use mind maps to create field notes, as these may allow for different ways of expressing what is happening in the classroom. For additional frameworks for field notes, take a look at Bernard's (2011) chapter on the topic.

ACTIVITY 7.5

Use the notetaking/notemaking method to take notes on part of a class session (yours or another teachers'). See the example below. Did you find this useful? Why? Why not? Did you find this easy or difficult?

Notetaking/Notemaking Example:

Research Question: In what ways do quieter students interact with talkative students during classroom activities?

Operationalized Components: quieter, quieter students, talkative, talkative students, classroom activities

Table 7.1   'Notetaking and Notemaking'

Notetaking	Notemaking
Students working in groups on grammar exercise	Are they all engaged in the task? Why are a couple students quiet?
Lecture with teacher in front, about the grammar topic	Student who was quiet during group work asked a question – is he less comfortable when talking with a particular classmate?

When you create a structure for your field notes, keep in mind that you will want them to be easily searchable and analysable once you get to the analysis phase. Therefore, you need to balance their being emergent based on what you are finding while also adhering to particular structures so that they are easy to use for your own analytical purposes. You can also try other notetaking methods, some of which you may be teaching to your own students. I would recommend that you try out different approaches the first few times, to see what works best for you. And then return to your approach later in the process, asking yourself if it is still working for you or not.

Collecting Artefacts

An additional component of ethnography involves collecting relevant artefacts (e.g., items from the classroom and students' papers), which can provide you with additional information about the patterns you are noticing in the other data collection methods you are using. This process may also involve collecting artefacts outside of the classroom setting (e.g. playground, cafeteria). In addition, visual media can be a compelling form of collecting and sharing data, as they can be accessible to and understandable for individuals from a variety of cultural and linguistic backgrounds. Increasingly, researchers are finding that visual approaches can reach and make their research relevant to wider audiences.

Mapping

As discussed above, ethnography allows you as the researcher to understand the 'culture' of your classroom over time. In addition to observing and taking notes of student–teacher interactions, student–student interactions and language use, you can create maps of the physical environment that shape these interactions. Mapping highlights the ways that the built and material environment is not simply the context where interactions happen but also part of the interactions themselves (cf. Goodwin, 2007; Scollon and Scollon, 2003). For example, it might be important that you have set up the tables in your classroom in a particular way (cf. Harmer, 2007), as this allowed students in different groups to interact with one another. It may be difficult to describe in words how the room was set up, but a map can tell that story quite easily. Maps can be hand-drawn, created using computer programmes, or created online. The most important thing is that the maps can help you remember the room setup when you look back at them later and that they help someone reading your research understand better what was happening during a particular interaction.

ACTIVITY 7.6

Choose a day this week and can create a hand-drawn map of your classroom at the beginning of the day and again at the end of the day. Then write some notes explaining how/why the parts of the room changed/moved throughout the day. How might this create and/or connect to a research interest of yours?

Photography

Another way that you can capture the visual aspects of your classroom is through photography. It is essential that you get students' and parents' permission to take photographs for your research, which may go beyond the consent forms that they already filled out for the school/institution. Also make sure to talk with your institution's administration about this before beginning your research. An important idea in photography is framing, in which you select how much/what you want to include in the picture. You can even use your phone to take photos, using some of the tips here (http://www.nationalgeographic.com/photography/photo-tips/iphone-photography-tips/).

Continuous Monitoring

Continuous monitoring is a research methodology in which you 'watch a person, or group of people and record their behaviour as faithfully as possible' (Bernard, 2011, p 306). For example, you could select particular students on whom you will do 'focal follows' (Bernard, 2011, p. 306) during a discrete period of time and/or at particular time intervals (for an example, see Bernard, 2011, p. 307). Following particular students for set amounts of time can allow you to make arguments focused on patterns related to what those students are doing, when they are doing it and how much of it they are doing. Perhaps in your research you are interested in what students at particular proficiency levels do during group work. Continuous monitoring would be a great method for that kind of research question. You will need to create 'codes' for the behaviour of interest – for example, 'looking up', 'talking in L1 with student', 'raising hand', etc. The 'codes' may become more granular/detailed depending upon your particular interests, which can become more specific over time (even if they started as inductive/open-ended).

ACTIVITY 7.7

Which categories of student would you want to use continuous monitoring for? What behaviours are you interested in? What codes might you use?

Audio-Recording

One aspect of observation and ethnography is recording, which will provide you with data that can be viewed multiple times and analysed from multiple standpoints. You might audio-record students during particular classroom activities that are of interest to you (e.g. student presentations, role plays).

Frequently audio-recording is perceived as less invasive than video-recording and therefore less face threatening. Students may therefore be more willing to consent to being audio-recorded, so it is important to consider some of the ethical issues involved. For example, one essential ethical issue with audio-recording is that the participants know in advance that you will be audio-recording them, that you have their consent to be recorded and that they know for what purposes you might use the recordings. There are also key methodological questions involve in audio-recording, for example where it should be placed and how you keep track of who spoke when. You do want to place the recording device in a place where it can pick up as much sound as possible, without the recording device becoming distracting to the participants.

Video-Recording

Video-recording is another effective method that can be used to capture naturalistic interactions (Heath, Hindmarsh and Luff, 2010), including classroom discourse, interviews and focus groups. Here again it is important to keep in mind the ethics of recording, especially when recording your own students. Keeping ethics in mind is especially true if you use recording for other purposes in class (e.g. for presentations in oral skills courses). Video-recordings can provide you with rich data that can be returned to multiple times in the future. They allow you to examine the details of language-in-interaction, through discourse and content analysis. In online classroom environments, you may choose to record asynchronous sessions (e.g. on Adobe Connect) and then you will be able to analyse that data later on. You might also have students create their own video-recordings, which you can then analyse as it relates to your research interests.

Student-Created Visuals

In addition to using visual approaches to data collection, you can also have students create visuals in class that you can then use as data. For example, you might use an online resource (e.g, polleverywhere.com) to create a poll that you share with the students and a word cloud would be created from that. You can then analyse that word cloud for patterns related to your research interest (e.g. grammatical accuracy). You could also have students create a visual of a key concept in your content-based language classroom and you can then analyse those visuals for patterns. Another way to do this might be to teach the genre of memes and then have students create memes in class about a particular concept, which you then analyse. All of these are engaging ways for students to express themselves in visual and linguistic ways, which can then provide compelling data for your research project.

For example, in my TESOL/TFL courses, I have had students interview language learners and create VIVID pictures (http://www.danroam.com/assets/pdf/tools/BBB_grammar.pdf) of those learners' stories. You can then analyse those VIVID pictures for patterns related to students' histories (for an example, see https://vimeo.com/126705517). These are a small example of digital storytelling (http://digitalstorytelling.coe.uh.edu/), which combines forms of digital media with storytelling. Digital storytelling can be a very effective way for students from diverse backgrounds to share their stories, be creative and learn genre conventions. One approach is to have students watch a digital story without the sound and then imagine what the story is about. Then they can create their own digital stories based on experiences they had in their home countries and/or those while they are in a new location. These digital stories can prove to be very fruitful data for your research, based on students' language ability, cultural backgrounds, histories, experiences, fluency and accuracy. For compelling examples of students' visual data, see Choi's (2016) *Creative Criticality in Multilingual Texts*. See also Saldana (2015, p. 126–129) for guidance on 'thinking visually' and again Saldana (2009, p. 79) for an example of an 'illustrated process for spreading rumors'. Collecting visual data can provide a rich complement to other forms of data collection and highlight aspects of your classroom that otherwise may not have become foci in your inquiry.

Data Sharing

Once you have collected your data, you will want to present it to a wide range of audiences (including students and fellow faculty members). One way to do this is to create an infographic using one of the many freely available online tools (e.g., http://piktochart.com), which can capture complex ideas in an easy-to-understand visual format. This can be a very useful way to communicate your ideas, especially when students have a range of proficiency levels. You may also use iMovie or other tools to create subtitles so that you can share your data with various audiences (https://www.wondershare.com/subtitle/subtitle-editor.html). You can also use 'frame grabs', which create pictures from particular frames in the video. This can help to highlight particular aspects of your argument: in publications, conference papers and workshop presentations.

ACTIVITY 7.8

What might be some visual ways that you could share your research with diverse audiences? How specifically would you represent your research visually?

Suggested Readings

Agar, M.H. (1996). *The Professional Stranger: An Informal Introduction to Ethnography*.
This book provides a useful starting point for the disposition and practice of ethnography, encouraging you to ask questions throughout the process of ethnographic inquiry.

Campbell Galman, S. (2007). *Shane, The Lone Ethnographer: A Beginner's Guide to Ethnography*. AltaMira Press.
This helpful handbook for ethnography is written in a graphic novel format, allowing you to grasp key concepts while doing hands-on activities. This is especially useful for novice researchers

and those who appreciate a visual approach to pedagogy. This could be appropriate as well if you want to teach your students ethnographic methods for any reason e.g. having them observe naturally occurring interactions to grasp descriptive language norms).

https://education.ucf.edu/mirc/docs/pp/FlaRE%20Professional%20Paper%20-%20Ethnographic%20Research.pdf
This short resource provides basic concepts and questions to consider before engaging in ethnographic research.

Online Resources

Case Studies:
https://www.tesol.org/read-and-publish/journals/tesol-quarterly/tesol-quarterlyresearch-guidelines/qualitative-research-case-study-guidelines

Mind Maps:
http://www.mindmapping.com/mind-mapping-in-education.php

Framing on iPhones:
http://www.upb.pitt.edu/uploadedFiles/Note%20Taking%20Techniques.pdf
http://iphonephotographyschool.com/composition-tips/

Classroom Maps:
http://classroom.4teachers.org/

Creating Subtitles:
https://www.wondershare.com/subtitle/subtitle-maker.html

8 Transcription: Process and Product

Guiding Questions:

yes!

1. Have you ever transcribed language? For what purposes?
2. Did you enjoy the transcription process? Why? Why not?
3. Do you ever read transcripts? If so, of what?
4. What might be some pros and cons for different transcription conventions?
5. How might you use the transcripts you create?

Introduction

This chapter will highlight the process of transcription, which you can use for a variety of purposes as a step towards coding, discourse analysis and/or content analysis. You can transcribe audio- and video-recordings of interviews, focus groups and interactions. Transcription is an intermediate step between the phases of data collection and analysis and it involves analytical decision making as well. In addition to using transcripts in your research, you can create transcripts of in-class interactions, technology-facilitated interactions and real-life interactions as a way to teach descriptive language norms to your class. You can also have students create transcripts of their own language use to heighten their awareness of linguistic patterns. Creating the transcription yourself can become a critical part of your overall research process since you become especially sensitive to the details of language and interaction. This may also help you later on to ascertain patterns within the data. However, transcription can take a great deal of time and effort. There may be research funding available such that you can hire a research assistant to help you with this task. In addition, it may not be necessary for you to transcribe absolutely all of your data for every research project. You can potentially be more selective about which recordings you need or want to transcribe and for what purposes in your research.

Transcription

As language teachers we recognize the importance of the details of language-in-interaction. It is in the details of language that meaning is created and communicated. An important research method that we can therefore appreciate is transcription, of written and spoken language. The *process* of transcribing allows us to become sensitive to the particular linguistic features of interest in our research. The *product* of transcribing provides us with tools to review and return to multiple times over the course of our research, to analyse patterns in relation to our research interests and questions. Before beginning transcription, it is important to determine the purposes for and uses of the transcripts. Will only you be analysing the transcripts? Will you share the transcripts with others? Do those people need to be familiar with particular transcription conventions in order to follow your argument? Once you have decided on these issues, then you can begin the transcription process. The most common use of transcription is for spoken language, but it can also be used to collect written genres for later analysis. For example, I undertook research on the use of modals in weather reports and therefore needed to create a small corpus of written transcriptions of online weather reports (discussed in more detail below). The process of collecting and organizing this data allowed me to more easily identify patterns in the data and make strong arguments. I was also able to include direct quotes from the data in the eventual write-up and presentation of my research, which I encourage you to do as well.

ACTIVITY 8.1

Identify a research question that would involve transcribing spoken or written language. Is this an inductive research question or a deductive research question?

Transcription Process

The process of transcription allows us to perceive the various details of interaction. Every choice we make in transcribing is an analytical one, meaning that there are no 'objective' transcripts (Bucholtz, 1999; Bucholtz and DuBois, n.d.; Duranti, 2006; Ochs, 1979; Schegloff, 2007). They represent our cultural and linguistic biases (e.g. reading from left to right and our research interests. Therefore, it is important to consider what might be the essential elements that should be included in any transcript. Bucholtz and DuBois (n.d.) provides a useful framework for determining the most important features to focus on in any transcript, which include words, word sequence, speaker change, turn sequence, intonation unit and speaker label. The next level up ('basic') would also include pauses, marginal words, laughter, overlap start and end and unit sequence. Below I will discuss in detail the process of transcribing spoken inter-action. Later in the chapter, I will treat written discourse transcription as well.

ACTIVITY 8.2

Read through the possible transcription conventions at the following links. Which of the linguistic features in the list would you include in a transcript of your classroom interactions? Why?
http://www.linguistics.ucsb.edu/projects/transcription/A02bsymbols.pdf (organized into four 'levels of delicacy': preliminary, basic, boundary, interaction)
http://www.linguistics.ucsb.edu/projects/transcription/A04comparison.pdf

Transcription Example

Read through the transcript in the Appendix, taken from Avineri, 2012. It is from a Yiddish university-level classroom. You may notice that the transcript includes words, intonation, pauses, emphasis, overlaps, nonverbal communication and volume. There are a number of analytical questions highlighted by the transcription choices I made. First, all of the names are pseudonyms, which is highlighted in the transcript itself. Second, by including certain nonverbal communication (and not others), I am making an implicit analytical claim that particular gestures are relevant to the analysis (and others are not). I chose not to include translations of the Yiddish words, since the interaction itself involves metalinguistic commentary. In terms of orthographic choices, I chose what I believed would make sense to English speakers while also remaining true to standard Yiddish transliteration. In addition, I chose at line 12 to write 'laughter' instead of writing out the details of the laughter itself (e.g. hehehuhuh). In every case, as the analyst I had a range of choices in terms of how I wanted to represent the interaction, all of which were shaped by my interests and goals. This highlights the fact that there is no 'objective' transcript, though we can try our best to remain as true as possible to the interaction itself.

Transcription Steps

When creating a transcription, I recommend that you go through the following seven steps: (1) listening to the recording, (2) creating a SPEAKING model, (3) selecting relevant portions of the interaction to transcribe, (4) getting your bearings, (5), transcribing using a selected set of transcription conventions, (6) considering whether your eventual analysis will be content analysis ('what') and/or discourse analysis ('how') and (7) including as much detail as possible.

Listening to the Recording

Research based on spoken language may include monologues (e.g. presidential speeches, student presentations, students' oral reflections) and/or interaction (e.g. TV shows, students' classroom interactions, interviews, focus groups). Generally speaking, transcription is used as part of an inductive set of research methods. Therefore, it is important that you listen to the entire recording (or recordings) in an open-ended way, to get a good sense of the speakers, turns being taken, topics and potential themes in the interaction(s). This is especially true when transcribing an interaction in which you were involved (e.g. interview, classroom interaction), as the transcription process helps move you from participant in the interaction to observer of the interaction. While listening to the recording, you can use the SPEAKING model (http://www1.appstate.edu/~mcgowant/hymes.htm) as a starting point in terms of the details: setting, participants, ends, act sequences, key, instrumentalities, norms and genres. You may need to listen to the recording a couple of times in order to have enough information to complete an effective SPEAKING model. While listening to the recording, you can also take notes about what happens, including timestamps at regular intervals or at salient moments and make other relevant notes for your later reference.

ACTIVITY 8.3

Complete the SPEAKING model in your classroom on a particular day. What did you realize upon completing this activity in terms of the details of your classroom?

ACTIVITY 8.4

What is an example of a research question that would use interactions on TV shows as data? What is an example of a research question that would use students' presentations as data?

One important thing to keep in mind is the fact that you can reasonably make arguments only about the type of transcription data you are analysing. Therefore, you cannot make a general argument about question design in naturally occurring Spanish based only on the ways that questions are asked on scripted Spanish TV shows.

Selecting the Relevant Portion(s)

Once you have a sense of what is happening in the recording as a whole, you can then select a portion of the overall recording that you believe will be fruitful in terms of your research focus. I would recommend that you start with two to three minutes of the recording as a starting place. One reason you might select a portion is that the participants whose language you are most interested in are speaking during that section. Another reason might be that the topic you are interested in exploring is being discussed during that section. If you are interested in particular grammatical features, you may also find that a particular section includes those features used frequently by the participants. For example, perhaps your research interest is focused on the use of modals (e.g. 'will', 'might') in TV weather reports so that you can teach these patterns to your students. You may collect ten recordings of weather reports and then listen to two or three of them. You can then decide when modals are used most and then only transcribe those portions for later analysis.

Once you have decided on a relevant section, you can then transcribe that portion in detail. You may then select other portions of the recording that you would like to transcribe in detail as well. This may be because they provide more depth on the relevant features or topics of interest, or perhaps because they complement the selected portion in another way that is connected to your research interest.

Getting Your Bearings

When preparing to transcribe spoken discourse, you should begin by listening to the first 10–15 seconds of the recording a few times without writing anything down. This will allow you to get a good sense of the speakers' voices, pace and general topics. In the first few rounds you can then write down at least who the speakers are and the words they used so that you have something on the page. Then, during subsequent 'listens', you can begin to add additional details that you believe may be relevant to your analysis. It is generally better to include more details than you think you will need so that you have as much as possible on which to base your analysis. I would recommend that you select a set of transcription conventions at the beginning and do your best to stick with that throughout the process: http://www.linguistics. ucsb.edu/projects/transcription/representing.

ACTIVITY 8.5

Find an already transcribed video online (e.g. from YouTube) that is of interest to you, ideally with more than one person speaking. Practise going through the transcription steps described above and then compare your transcription (at least the words) to the transcription provided on YouTube. How did the process go? What might you change in your process in the future?

Written Transcriptions

In some cases, your research may involve detailed analysis of written texts (e.g. newspapers, reports, literacy materials). For example, you might be interested in examining in depth the way that newspaper headlines use (or do not use) definite and indefinite articles, in order to create lessons for your students based on these descriptive norms. In cases like these, it is important that you be systematic and selective in terms of how you collect the data (e.g. timeframe, number of newspapers, focus of the headlines). You might collect all newspaper headlines from the front page of the same newspaper for a period of two weeks. You might collect all newspaper headlines from page five of three different newspapers for a period of one week. You might collect newspaper headlines about the same event from the same day from ten different newspapers. All of these are reasonable ways to approach the collection of written data. The most important thing to keep in mind is that your data collection approach is systematic and selective and has a particular rationale that is closely connected to your research questions.

Transcripts of Interviews

You can also create transcripts of the data discussed in Chapter 6 (from interviews, focus groups), since you will generally record these for later data analysis. If you are planning to engage in content analysis of the interviews or focus groups, focused primarily on the 'what' that was stated, then you might select a simpler set of transcription conventions (e.g. including only participants, words). However, if you imagine that you may engage in discourse analysis, focused primarily on the 'how' (e.g. turn design, linguistic features), then your set of transcription conventions may include more detail (e.g. intonation, pauses, overlaps). These are decisions you can make based on your particular interests and goals. Generally speaking, it is better to include more detail than less, which can allow you to analyse whatever may become salient. Also, as mentioned above, the process of transcription itself can bring linguistic details to your awareness when otherwise you may not have noticed them.

Translations

Depending upon the purposes and audiences for your transcription, you may also include translations of the transcription text. This introduces a number of additional analytical choices, as highlighted here: https://jalt.org/pansig/2003/HTML/Greer.htm. Orthographic symbols for different languages vary of course; therefore, it is important to read samples of transcripts with the languages in your data.

Students' Transcriptions

awesome idea!

You can teach your students how to transcribe their own language as a way to heighten awareness of their language use patterns and perhaps improve them. In conversation courses I have taught in the past, this has proven to be a very useful way to have students realize the details of their language use. You can share with them the possible transcription conventions and allow them, for example, to choose five that they wish to include in their transcripts. In many cases, through this activity they realize specific issues related to their vocabulary use, pauses and grammar. At first this can be difficult or embarrassing for students, but soon afterwards the majority of students realize the value of engaging in transcription for this purpose.

Conclusion

Transcription is a valuable step between data collection and analysis, which can allow you to notice the particular details of language use in your classroom and in the world more broadly. As noted above, this intermediate step also involves a number of analytical choices that can shape the data you will eventually analyse. These detailed records of real-life language use can provide you with valuable data about classroom interactions, real-life language use and students' linguistic strengths and areas for improvement. Once you have your transcriptions, you can begin the process of discourse analysis or content analysis, which will be described in detail in Chapter 10.

Suggested Reading

http://www.maxwell.syr.edu/uploadedFiles/moynihan/cqrm/Newsletter2.1.pdf
This is a useful online newsletter with detailed information about various approaches to the analysis of qualitative data.

9 Approaches to Collection of Quantitative Data

Guiding Questions:

1. Do you prefer to process information in numbers or in words?
2. Do you have theories about why certain students perform better than others in your classroom? How might you collect data to test those theories?
3. Do you ever read about experiments in the media?
4. Do you find experimental research convincing? Why? Why not?
5. What are some ethical issues raised by conducting experimental research with human subjects?

Introduction

This chapter discusses approaches to the collection of quantitative data for examining individual and community practices and ideologies (for further exploration, see Plonsky, 2015). We will discuss different quantitative research designs, variables, levels of measurement, reliability, validity, replicability and sampling. These will be discussed as they connect to deductive research questions.

Research Using Quantitative Data in Language Teaching

Until this point, this book has focused primarily on qualitative data and interpretive approaches to examining language teaching in classrooms. Underpinning these methods is frequently an open-ended worldview that allows for patterns to emerge in your process of inquiry. In this chapter, we will focus on ways to collect data that are numeric and measurable and they are therefore more easily comparable across individuals. Frequently, this approach is connected to a deductive research question that begins with a set of theories about relationships among variables, which your research seeks to confirm or disconfirm.

There are numerous cases in which a more deductive approach is a better fit for your research questions. In these cases, you may start with a hypothesis that you seek to confirm or disconfirm. For example, perhaps you are interested in finding out how students perform on grammar tests when you give them immediate individual corrective feedback in class. In order to examine a question like this, it will be necessary for you to compare/contrast the performance of students in your class, putting them into different groups. You would then collect data of these different groups' performance and draw conclusions based on those data.

Example Research Questions

You may remember from Chapter 3 that deductive research questions begin with theories or hypotheses and then look at particular cases to see how they relate to these theories or hypotheses. Frequently they are focused on answering yes or no (vs how) since they are attempting to confirm or disconfirm the hypotheses that are shaping your research. Below are a few examples of research questions of this type:

1. Do intermediate-level Mandarin learners learn characters faster when they practise with classmates?

2. Do videos played during class have an effect on Spanish students' acquisition of preterit and imperfect?
3. Do synchronous online lessons affect students' acquisition of question formation in English?
4. What is the relationship between task-based language teaching and grammatical accuracy? (This one is somewhat more open-ended than the previous three examples, but it still assumes a relationship between the two variables.)

Types of Research Involving Quantitative Data

There are numerous approaches to quantitative research (Phakiti, 2015). The most well-known is **experimental research**, in which the researcher manipulates the research setting in some way to best understand the relationships among variables. In **quasi-experimental research**, it is not practical or ethical to have a random sample. Therefore, there are some elements of experimental design but not all. Cause and effect may be more difficult to determine, but it can be inferred. **Correlational research** also determines the relationships among variables, without manipulating the research setting. **Causal-comparative research** (Gay, Mills and Arasian, 2011) is similar to correlational research, but the goal is to determine cause and effect among variables. **Survey research** can involve quantitative measures, based on particular question types. **Cross-sectional research** compares and contrasts different groups at the same time, which allows you to examine similar groups without having to wait for them to change. **Longitudinal research** involves in-depth analysis of the same group over time, which was discussed in Chapter 6 in relation to ethnography. **Cross-sequential research** involves analysing different groups longitudinally over time and also comparing and contrasting them.

Variables

An essential component of experimental research design is variables, which are measurable and observable means of capturing the phenomena of interest. There are three main types of variables. **Independent/Experimental/Predictor variables** are those variables over which the researcher has some control. **Dependent/Outcome variables** are those variables that are affected in some way by the manipulation of the Independent/Experimental/Predictor variables. A **Confounding/Moderator variable** is a variable that may have an impact on your findings, though you may not be able to predict it in advance. For example, if your research question is 'How do teacher recasts impact students' oral test scores?', the independent variable is 'teacher recasts' and the dependent variable is 'oral test scores'. It is possible that you find out that the age of students affects their oral test scores, even though this was not one of your original research interests. Acknowledging the possibility of a moderator variable at the beginning of your research process can allow you to answer the question: How do you know if any differences between the two groups is due to the treatment and not to something else? All of the research designs listed above can help you determine learner differences because they assume that teaching interventions will have diverse effects on learners of different groups.

ACTIVITY 9.1

What are some variables you are interested in your language classroom? Do you have any hunches/educated guesses about the relationships among these different variables? How might you shape those interests into a deductive research question?

Levels of Measurement

There are four levels of measurement in quantitative data: nominal, ordinal, interval and ratio (http://www.social researchmethods.net/kb/measlevl.php), discussed here in order of level of measurement. **Nominal (also called categorical)** means that you assign numbers randomly to different instances; the numbers themselves have no meaning. For example, '1' would be for biology major and '2' for comparative literature major. But the numbers themselves have no importance (i.e. a biology major is not double a comparative literature major). This would include dichotomous results, which would be quantitative data collected primarily through questionnaires (e.g. full- or part-time enrolment). **Ordinal (also called ranked)** means that the results can be ordered in some way. For example, you might code ordinal measures for language training as 0 = no college-level training, 1 = passing some college-level language classes, 2 = post-college-level training. But the difference between 0 and 1 and between 1 and 2 is not equal. With ordinal measures, the interval between values is not interpretable.

Interval measures mean that there is interpretable meaning in the distance between attributes. For example, if we choose to code time of day, then the difference between each attribute could be equal (between 11 a.m. and noon is the same as between 3 p.m. and 4 p.m.). It is therefore possible to calculate the average of interval measures. There is debate about whether Likert scale responses can reasonably be analysed using interval measures (Suskie, 2009) since it is possible that there is a difference in the spread between 'strongly agree' and 'agree' and between 'disagree' and 'strongly disagree'. **Ratio** measures are similar to interval measures, except that there is a natural zero. For example, if you use a ratio measure, you can reasonably say that you had twice as many students this semester as last semester. Another example of a ratio measure is age. Interval and ratio data are both examples of **scaled** data. Generally speaking, it is preferable to include higher levels of measurement, as opposed to lower orders of measurement. This allows you to make stronger arguments in the long run.

Reliability, Validity and Replicability

Two important concepts in quantitative research are reliability and validity. Reliability can be thought of as consistency (Suskie, 2009). Interrater reliability ensures that anyone who see or analyses your data would come to the same conclusions. Intrarater reliability means that the same person would provide the same score or measure no matter when they analyse the data and no matter whose data they are analysing. Validity means that you are measuring what you are seeking to measure. There are three types of validity: construct, internal and external (Balnaves and Caputi, 2001, p. 89). Construct validity is 'the extent to which your constructs are successfully operationalized and represent the phenomenon you want to study' (p. 89). Internal validity is 'the extent to which your research design really allows you to draw conclusions about the relationship between variables' (p. 89). External validity is 'the extent to which your sample is genuinely representative of the population from which you have drawn it' (p. 89). For an explanation of different types of validity, take a look at this useful resource: http://www. socialresearchmethods.net/kb/measval.php. It is also important for studies that include quantitative data to demonstrate replicability (Brown, 2004, p. 492), which 'requires researchers to provide enough information about a study to allow other researchers to replicate or repeat the study exactly as it was originally conducted'. Some of the information that you can provide to ensure replicability would include participants, instruments and procedures (Brown, 2004, p. 492).

Sampling

As noted above, external validity is predicated on the notion that your sample is representative of the population you would like to make generalizations about. You may remember that sampling was discussed in relation to questionnaires. Generally speaking, random samples are reserved for experimental research, while other types of sampling can be used for the other research designs listed above. In descriptive statistics you are primarily interested in the sample itself (as opposed to a larger population you are attempting to generalize about). However, in order to perform inferential statistics, it is important that your sample have the potential to be generalizable (cf. http://biostat.mc.vanderbilt.edu/wiki/pub/Main/ClinStat/Basic. inference.pdf). This means that the sample should be representative of a group larger than itself. It is best to have a larger sample size when possible, as you can make stronger arguments as a result. For additional guidance on statistical reasoning, see Dietz and Kalof (2009).

Experimental Research Details

There are a range of approaches in the experimental method (for a description of these options, see Nunan and Bailey, 2009, chapter 4). If you are interested in undertaking an experimental research design, one option is for you to create 'treatment' and 'non-treatment' groups. The 'treatment' group is the group who would receive a particular type of intervention of interest (e.g. additional computer time, discussion time in groups). The 'non-treatment' group would not receive this intervention. You would then measure the differences (if any) between the two groups' test scores and build an argument based on the details of your experimental design. This particular example would be called a pretest-posttest design, since you will provide students with a pre-test (before the intervention) and post-test (after the intervention). In experimental studies, you may therefore be interested in effects over time, which makes them longitudinal as well. You are looking for a quantitative difference between the two groups.

Parametric and Non-Parametric Data

Another important distinction in quantitative data collection is that between parametric and non-parametric data (http://changingminds.org/explanations/research/analysis/parametric_non-parametric.htm). Parametric data assumes in advance that the distribution of the data is normal and that the variance between individuals or groups is homogeneous. Typical data is ratio or interval. For non-parametric data there could be any distribution to the data and typical data is ordinal or nominal. You may have noticed that parametric research uses data that is at a higher level of measurement, while non-parametric research uses data that is at a lower level of measurement. Though one can draw more conclusions with parametric data, non-parametric data is simpler (and therefore easier to start with) (Turner, 2014).

Ethical Considerations

In the collection of qualitative data, it may be difficult to predict how research participants might interact with you, which can raise a host of ethical questions and dilemmas. Quantitative data collection, through its more controlled nature, involves different ethical questions. For example, it is important that the sampling process be ethical in terms of who is chosen and who is not part of the research study. You will also want to ensure in experimental research that the treatment or intervention itself does not cause undue harm or anxiety to the research participants. As discussed in Chapter 4, it is essential to consider potential ethical issues in advance of beginning and throughout the process of data collection and analysis.

Additional Uses for Quantitative Data Collection

There are other uses for quantitative data collection, some of which connect to qualitative data discussed previously. For example, you may be able to approach observations in a quantitative manner (e.g. counting the number of times that students ask for clarification during one class session). Continuous monitoring could be approached in a quantitative way, by counting a range of student behaviours in the classroom. You could then create a numeric representation of student practices and interactions. **Corpora**, small or large collections of naturally occurring spoken or written data analysable in the form of written transcripts, can also be analysed in quantitative ways (e.g. finding how many times a particular verb and preposition collocate in X number of newspaper articles). Corpus analysis (http://www.essex.ac.uk/linguistics/external/clmt/w3c/corpus_ling/content/introduction.html) can be used in combination with more qualitative approaches (e.g., coding, discourse analysis, content analysis).

Conclusion

This chapter provided you with terminology, concepts and approaches necessary to engage in quantitative data collection that may be useful for your research questions. You can use these data collection techniques on their own, in combination with one another, or in combination with qualitative data. These choices depend entirely on the research questions you are attempting to answer with one type or multiple types of data. Once you have these data, you can begin the data analysis process, which may include frequency distributions, percentage distributions, descriptive statistics and/or inferential statistics (with the assistance of online tools in many cases) (to be discussed in Chapter 11).

Suggested Readings

http://study.com/academy/lesson/research-designs-quasi-experimental-case-studies-correlational.html
This straightforward online video provides clear descriptions and distinctions (with visuals) for different types of psychometric research designs. There is also a quiz in case you want to make sure that the various approaches are clear to you.

https://statistics.laerd.com
This useful resource provides information about basic key concepts in statistics, including variable types and descriptive vs inferential statistics. In order to access all of its functionalities, you need to pay for a subscription.

http://www.socialresearchmethods.net/kb/measlevl.php
This online resource provides basic information about levels of measurement, which is necessary for the effective analysis of quantitative data.

http://psc.dss.ucdavis.edu/sommerb/sommerdemo/scaling/levels.htm
This is another useful online tool with clear guidance on levels of measurement for analysis of quantitative data.

Section III: Data Analysis

10 Interpretive Analysis of Qualitative Data

Guiding Questions:

1. What are the different types of qualitative data you have collected?
2. How might you organize this data?
3. Which data type would you like to analyse first? Why?
4. What do you think are the most appropriate ways to analyse that data?
5. What are some systems that you can set up to analyse your data in ways that are intuitive to your ideal process?

Introduction

In this chapter, we will discuss interpretive analysis of qualitative data, in particular the process of grounded theory building as it relates to inductive research. We will focus on selecting the appropriate data analysis method (e.g. coding, discourse analysis, content analysis) for identifying patterns and themes in the particular data you have collected. We will then discuss some steps for engaging in these different qualitative data analysis methods. These approaches to selection and procedure will serve you well as practitioner-researchers as you work through qualitative data collected in a variety of ways. Your ability to bring different kinds of analysis and interpretation together will allow you to identify and create theories about how things work in your classroom. We will approach the chapter going from macro-level to micro-level data analysis (starting with thematic coding and moving to discourse analysis), in relation to various kinds of qualitative data (questionnaires, interviews, focus groups, reflections, observations, recordings, transcriptions and maps).

Description vs Analysis vs Interpretation

Description involves providing in-depth details – 'thick description' (Geertz, 1973) – of the who, what, where and when of your data. Analysis is 'data close' and should be focused on determining patterns and themes in your data. The strength of the data analysis can make or break your argument and its potential for convincing your audience.

The interpretation of your data is one step beyond analysis (Bailey, 2007, p. 175), moving you to provide answers to 'why', allowing you to entertain multiple possibilities for why the data looks as it does. You move beyond your particular data to make conjectures, synthesize and connect your findings to existing literature. Wolcott (1994) highlights that the goal of interpretation is 'to reach out for understanding or explanation beyond the limits of what can be explained with the degree of certainty usually associated with analysis' (pp. 10–11). Interpretation of the analytical material is the time when 'researchers draw inferences, use theory for insights, raise questions, make comparisons and provide personal reactions. … [It] requires hunches, insights and intuition (Creswell, 1998; Wolcott, 1994)' (Bailey, 2007, p. 177). Interpretation generally happens towards the end of a researcher's process and allows the researcher to demonstrate the ways in which their analysis may be relevant to their target audiences (Bailey, 2007, p. 177). Thinking interpretively is important because it '1. Develops highdeep levels of reflection and highdeep forms of writing, 2. Prods you into extending beyond your particular research study towards more general applications,

3. Motivates thinking towards conceptual, abstract and theoretical domains and 4. Challenges you to consider the practical and utilitarian value of your work to others' (Saldana, 2015, p. 157). Implications are your opportunity to consider 'now what?' based on your analysis and interpretation.

A Reminder about Inductive Research

Inductive research is open-ended during data collection, such that you can allow themes and patterns to emerge organically. Once you are at the data analysis phase, you will be working to find those themes and patterns in ways that are consistent with the data at hand. Therefore, the data analysis phase is more closed-ended in your journey towards creating a theory. It is important that your data analysis process be systematic and clear to yourselves and to others and that it is consistently connected directly with your research questions. Qualitative data analysis can sometimes be subject to scrutiny from those who believe it is overly subjective (i.e. not 'verifiable' or objective in the ways that quantitative data analysis may seem to be). It is therefore preferable to engage in qualitative data analysis with someone else if possible, such that your intuitions can be checked against someone else's. The same issues of reliability are present in analysis of both qualitative and quantitative data. In the next section, we will discuss some approaches to beginning the process of analysis of qualitative data.

Steps for Interpretive Analysis

One way to ensure systematicity in your interpretive analysis of qualitative data is by following set steps very closely.

1. Make a catalogue of the entire dataset
2. Begin with one data type at a time (e.g. interviews)
3. Continue with the same data type (e.g. another questionnaire, another interview, another transcript)

4. Start with another data type
5. Continue with that data type
6. Begin comparing/contrasting across data types

Your first step will be to create a system of organizing your data that is intuitive, organized and searchable. You are the person who will be returning to your data to examine it in detail; therefore, you want to make sure that you can easily find the information you are looking for. By making a catalogue of your entire dataset, you are first quantifying your data by the number of videos, observations, pictures, maps, interviews and so on. You may also want to number each video, observation and so on so that you can easily refer back to them. You can then organize your data, broadly speaking, by who, what, where and when. This means that you can organize the data based on particular students, particular activities, or particular times of day, if you believe that any of these are relevant units of analysis. For example, you may have three observations of students engaging in roleplaying activities (WHAT) or three interviews of fellow teachers (WHO). I would also recommend organizing your data chronologically, not only because this is fairly straightforward but also because you may then be able to see the development of particular patterns over time. In the next section, I include some other possible ways to organize your data.

ACTIVITY 10.1

What are some other ways you can think of to organize your data that are intuitive, organized and searchable for you?

Making a Catalogue of the Entire Dataset

An important step in qualitative data analysis, which some researchers skip over, is creating a detailed catalogue of the entire dataset. This will help you create boundaries on how much data you have and of what type. Below are some ways that you can start to organize the different data you have:

Questionnaires

–By student (pseudonym)
–By date collected
–By class (if comparing/contrasting across different classes)

Interviews

–By date
–By interviewee

Reflections

–By teacher
–By student
–By date

Focus Groups

–By topic
–By date

Observations

–By date
–By setting
–By overall topics
–By overall activities

Recordings (audio, video)

–By date
–By setting
–By overall topics
–By overall activities
–By participants

Transcripts

–By date
–By setting
–By participants

Figure 10.1 Approaches to Organizing Your Data

The ways that you choose to organize your data is a first analytical step. For example, organizing reflections by date (though seemingly a logical and logistical choice) may implicitly demonstrate your belief that there has been change *over time*. Having the reflections organized by date would help you more easily track those changes.

Questions throughout the Interpretive Analysis Process

Though there are multiple interpretive data analysis methods, there are core questions we can ask ourselves no matter which particular method we select (toolkit.pellinstitute.org):

1. What patterns/common themes emerge around specific items in the data?
2. Are there any deviations from these patterns?
3. What interesting stories emerge from the data?
4. Do any of the patterns/emergent themes suggest that additional data needs to be collected?
5. Do the patterns that emerge support the findings of other corresponding qualitative analyses that have been conducted?

Kaplan-Weinger and Ullman (2015) provide a useful way of 'Looking at My Data' for ethnographic analysis in particular: focusing on practices, themes, norms and connections (p. 130).

Selecting the Appropriate Data Analysis Method(s)

Broadly speaking, the three main ways to analyse qualitative data are coding, content analysis and discourse analysis. Their uses are summarized in the table below. It may be appropriate to use multiple data analysis methods with the various types of data in your research study. You may use different methods with the same data as well. And the same analytical method (e.g. coding) has different consequences and issues to consider depending upon the data that it is being used to analyse. It is possible to use any of the three methods with all of the qualitative data you have collected, though the focus of the analysis will be different. To ensure research soundness and objectivity, where possible it is a good idea to have more than one person engage in analysis.

Table 10.1 Methods, Data Types and Analysis Purposes

Method	Used with	Used to analyse
Coding	Interviews, Observations, Open-Ended Responses, Written and Spoken Transcripts	Themes and Patterns
Content Analysis	Interviews, Observations, Open-Ended Responses, Written and Spoken Transcripts	'What' is expressed (e.g. categories, types)
Discourse Analysis	Interviews, Observations, Open-Ended Responses, Written and Spoken Transcripts	'How' something is expressed (e.g. linguistic features, turn design)

Content analysis is frequently used in interviews since there are generally only two people involved and one person is doing most of the talking. Discourse analysis is frequently used in interactional data (e.g. video-recordings of classroom inter-action, focus groups). See Bernard (2011) for further discussion of various forms of text analysis.

Coding

As discussed throughout the book, inductive research involves the emergence of themes over time. Therefore, coding is the most common form of qualitative data analysis. See Saldana, 2009, p. 12 for 'A streamlined codes-to-theory model for qualitative inquiry', highlighting the analytic moves from the particular to the general and from the real to the abstract. Coding involves an iterative process of noticing, collecting and thinking (Seidel, 1998) – reviewing data, taking notes and beginning to sort the data into categories, allowing you to create a 'framework of thematic ideas about it' (Gibbs, 2007) (http://betterevaluation.org/evaluation-options/thematiccoding). The main steps for thematic coding are as follows:

1. Familiarize yourself with the data (similar to what we discussed in relation to transcripts in Chapter 8)
2. Create initial codes
3. Search for themes
4. Review themes (look at data and see if they can fit into your themes)
5. Define and name themes

A code 'in qualitative inquiry is most often a word or short phrase that symbolically assigns a summative, salient, essence-capturing and/or evocative attribute for a portion of language-based or visual data' (Saldana, 2009, p. 3). There are two phases to thematic coding: **initial or open coding** (in which you use the examples to begin the process of creating themes) and closed or focused or axial coding (in which you use the open codes to begin to organize the examples) (Bailey, 2007, pp. 128–129; Strauss and Corbin, 1990). Memoing is also part of this process, 'the writing of memos to oneself regarding insights one derives from coding and reflecting on the data' (Bailey, 2007, p. 133). During the coding process, you can ask yourself the following open-ended questions:

1. What is going on?
2. What are people doing? What is the person saying?
3. What do these actions and statements take for granted?
4. How do structure and context serve to support, maintain, impede, or change these actions and statements? (Charmaz, 2003, pp. 94–5).

Codes should be as similar as possible to the other elements in the same group and as different as possible to elements in other groups. This has been referred to in the literature as 'lumping and splitting' (Saldana, 2009, p. 19). It is also important to remember that codes and themes are not the same thing. A theme is 'an *outcome* of coding, categorization and analytic reflection' (ibid., p. 13). As we engage in our initial processes of coding we are searching for short words or phrases that can explicitly connect back to the data (cf. Rossman and Rallis, 2003). These are then revisited during the subsequent coding and memoing phases as we look for more 'subtle and tacit processes' (Rossman and Rallis, 2003, p. 282) that we identify as themes.

ACTIVITY 10.2

What might be the strengths and limitations of coding?

One thing to keep in mind when coding is that you do not want your codes to end up being simply a list of the topics discussed in the interview, open-ended response and so on (for an effective example, see Figure 9.1 on p. 131 of Bailey, 2007). For example, when I first began coding a set of five person-centred interviews that I conducted with a Yiddish learner, my codes mapped onto topics that she discussed throughout the interviews (e.g. family life, linguistic proficiency). A further level of depth in coding would be to identify not just codes but themes (e.g. 'sense of belonging'). This distinction is also discussed in Gee (2014, pp. 71–72). Your goal is to create codes that build towards themes and eventually an argument, which is a discourse intended to persuade (Belcher, 2012). Very few people would be able to argue against a topic, but you will need to make a convincing case that the themes you have identified are salient (based on the examples that you share). 'First cycle' and 'second cycle' coding methods are discussed in detail in Saldana (2009), along with useful templates and examples.

Memoing is a key part of the coding process. Just below are some examples of the types of issues one can reflect on and write up during this phase (from Saldana, 2009, pp. 34–41):

1. how you personally relate to the participants and/or the phenomenon
2. your study's research questions
3. your code choices and their operational definitions
4. the emergent patterns, categories, themes and concepts
5. the possible networks (links, connections, overlaps, flows) among the codes, patterns, categories, themes and concepts
6. an emergent or related existing theory
7. any problems with the study
8. any personal or ethical dilemmas with the study
9. future directions for the study
10. the analytic memos generated thus far
11. the final report for the study

Interestingly, memos themselves can be coded and categorized (Saldana, 2009, pp. 41–42). Memos can also be used to analyse visual data (Saldana, 2009, pp. 42–44).

As mentioned above, the same data analysis method may pose particular issues when applied to specific data collection methods. For example, since focus groups involve multiple people, there will be more layers of analysis when engaging in the coding process. One way to handle this may be to start with micro-level discourse analysis and then move to macro-level coding for broader themes. In this way, focus groups are similar to video-recordings of classroom interaction. For recordings it would be important to read or watch the entire interaction and write notes with key ideas (including time stamps). You may then decide to transcribe only particular parts for further analysis.

In this section I will describe in some detail a possible coding process for questionnaires, to provide some guidelines that can be used for other data types as well. Once you have received your questionnaires from the respondents, you can begin the analysis process. First of all, you will want to read through the responses and see if any questionnaires were not completed or if certain responses were misinterpreted. Those questionnaires and/or responses may need to be disregarded in your overall analysis process. Next, you can begin to create a plan for analysis. What I outline below is a process that I recommend, but you can pick and choose from it or select a different order (as long as you have a clear rationale for your choices).

One way to begin your analysis of questionnaire data is with the more objective questions and then moving to more subjective questions. Therefore, you could begin with cataloguing and counting responses for demographic questions (e.g. age), dichotomous questions (e.g. yes/no) and then moving to rating questions (e.g. Likert scale). You can simply count the number of respondents who provided each type of response. Later in the process, you will begin to interpret the possible reasons for why they responded in those ways.

After going through these question types, you can move to the more subjective responses (e.g. open-ended questions, elaboration questions). This will involve looking for patterns. After focusing on open-ended questions, you can begin the 'question connection' process. This can involve looking at particular demographic questions (e.g. age, gender) as they may relate to types of responses. For example, you may notice that students from a particular country respond in a fairly consistent way to a question about technology. There may not be any relationship or interpretation to be made of this, but it is important to leave these possible connections open in the early stages of the analysis process. This may also include looking at how participants respond to different questions. For example, perhaps many of the students respond to a yes-no question with 'yes' when asked if they have taken four skills classes in the past and respond to a ranking question with 'strongly disagree' in relation to the idea that grammar drills help them in their current conversation class. It is possible that there is a relationship between these two pieces of information and therefore, these patterns should be noted during the analysis process.

Once you are at the stage when you can reasonably explore the responses to the open-ended questions, then you can begin the process of coding, as one way to begin searching for patterns and themes in your data. Since we are focused here on an inductive (emergent) approach to data analysis, we begin by reading through the responses in a very open way (without preconceived notions about what the themes and patterns might be). As described above, this involves two main stages: initial (open) and final (closed) coding. During the initial phase, you are creating broad categories based on the data in front of you. There is a nice example of how to do this here: https://www.academia.edu/709185/Analysing_and_presenting_qualitative_data. You first put 'tags' on the data based on the phenomena that continue to emerge in the responses. Then, as you continue reading the responses (and also connect those responses to other responses), you can fine-tune those 'tags' to make sure they are truly representative of the data in front of you.

There are a few important things to keep in mind in this regard. First of all, remember that coding is an iterative (ongoing) process. This means that the codes you start with may not be the ones that you end up with. Just because you think you have a pattern based on two responses does not mean that you should force other responses to fit that pattern. This means that you try out codes to see if they stick and then keep them or let them go. In addition, when reading responses, make sure you are alternating the order in which you read them. For example, if you have 20 questionnaire responses and you have numbered them #1–#20, make sure that when analysing responses to specific questions you sometimes read questionnaire #1 first and questionnaire #20 last and in other cases you go the other way around (or other orders). There is sometimes a tendency in coding to create themes based on the first few questionnaires, but it is important to view the same dataset from different vantage points to help ensure reliability. This can ensure that you do not get stuck with using one or two particular questionnaires as the starting points for your emerging codes. The themes you identify may not be present in every single questionnaire, but they are salient and/or frequent enough in the dataset to merit attention in your analysis. There are also times when one person's response is so striking that we include that in our analysis, even if it does not adhere to the themes or all the other questionnaires. This is fine, as long as there is a justification and rationale for including that response in particular.

Another issue to keep in mind in relation to the analysis process is the fact that sometimes you have too many questionnaires or too many responses to analyse for a particular purpose. For example, if you are working at a university and you are interested in giving questionnaires to all of the students enrolled in 1st-quarter Spanish, you may end up with too many questionnaires to reasonably analyse. This may mean that you select a subset of those questionnaires (e.g. 50 total), but it is important that you do not cherry-pick those questionnaires that fit something you want to say. You may select 25 males and 25 females (randomly and if those categories are relevant in some way to your research question) or perhaps the first 50 to respond (though those may be self-selecting subset of 'eager' respondents) or perhaps the first 25 to respond and the last 25 to respond (to deal with the issues just mentioned). For more information on analysing questionnaire data quantitatively, see Chapter 11. When considering what order you should write your analysis in, you can decide whether you will take a more discrete and micro-level approach (e.g. write about each question in turn, question types) or a more synthetic and macro-level approach (e.g. question connections, or themes). This is a decision you can make once you get to that stage of the process.

Coding frequently takes longer for interviews than for questionnaires since by their very nature they involve more open-ended questions that involve greater depth of analysis (and eventually, interpretation). I would recommend that you practise coding first based on one or two interviews, as opposed to trying to take on an entire set that is larger than that.

Content Analysis

Content analysis is focused on 'how' things are done in the world, in a way that is more descriptive than in discourse analysis. Through content analysis you can examine topics and words used in interviews, recordings and transcripts. There are two types of content analysis: conceptual analysis and relational analysis (http://writing.colostate.edu/guides/guide.cfm?guideid=61). In conceptual analysis you are looking for particular words and phrases that demonstrate a focus on certain topics (e.g. L1 transfer, thesis statements). In relational analysis you are looking for the ways that particular topics might be connected to other topics (e.g. L1 transfer and motivation, thesis statements and homework). Content analysis involves identifying words and phrases (describing), identifying themes and interpretation (http://toolkit.pellinstitute.org/evaluation-guide/analyse/analyse-qualitative-data/).

A more granular version of the steps of content analysis is included here for your reference (http://libweb.surrey.ac.uk/library/):

1. Copy and read through the transcript – make brief notes in the margin when interesting or relevant information is found.
2. Go through the notes made in the margins and list the different types of information found.
3. Read through the list and categorize each item in a way that offers a description of what it is about.
4. Identify whether or not the categories can be linked any way and list them as major categories (or themes) and / or minor categories (or themes).
5. Compare and contrast the various major and minor categories.
6. If there is more than one transcript, repeat the first five stages again for each transcript.
7. When you have done the above with all of the transcripts, collect all of the categories or themes and examine each in detail and consider if it fits and its relevance.

8. Once all the transcript data is categorized into minor and major categories/themes, review in order to ensure that the information is categorized as it should be.
9. Review all of the categories and ascertain whether some categories can be merged or if some need to them be sub-categorized.
10. Return to the original transcripts and ensure that all the information that needs to be categorized has been so.

Content analysis is a useful tool for analysing particular types of qualitative data, in order to ascertain the main topics and relationship between topics that are salient in your data.

ACTIVITY 10.3

Go through the ten steps above for an interview transcript in your data. Did you find the process easy or difficult? Do you think this will be a useful method for analysing the data you have in your study? Why? Why not?

Discourse Analysis

Discourse analysis (Gee, 2014; ten Have, 2007) is focused on how things are done in the world through language. This means that discourse analysts examine the particular naturalistic linguistic forms and features that were used to accomplish certain ends. As language teachers this is another method that we are especially suited for, since we have a detailed understanding of language-in-use and are accustomed to picking up on linguistic patterns in our language and that of our students'. In discourse analysis we consistently ask ourselves the question, 'why that now?' – meaning that we ask why a particular linguistic form is used in a particular context. There are multiple subtypes of discourse analysis, discussed in further detail in a range of sources (cf. Cameron and Panovic, 2014): **critical discourse analysis**, corpus-based discourse analysis, multimodal discourse analysis, computer-mediated discourse analysis and multilingual discourse analysis. You can also consider the ways that an ethnographic (cf. Philips, 2013) or sociolinguistic (cf. Wortham and Reyes, 2015) approach to your research can be combined with discourse analysis. In every case it is important to be systematic in your approach to the data so that you have sufficient data to back up your eventual claims. You can use discourse analysis for language teachers (cf. McCarthy, 1991) as a means to examine in-class interactions, technology-facilitated interactions (e.g. AdobeConnect) and real-life interactions that can be used to inform your own teaching and to teach descriptive language norms to your class. For example, you may choose to transcribe and conduct discourse analysis of videos thatyou will use for teaching.

Approaches to Discourse Analysis

Ten Have (2007) provides a four-step process for engaging in discourse analysis, examining turn-taking organization, sequence organization, repair organization and turn design. This is a macro- to micro-level approach, with turn-taking being focused on who says what when, whether there are overlaps and pauses and how much each participants speaks. Sequence organization focuses on how one thing leads to another, for example how greetings move into small talk moves into discussion of a particular topic moves into another topic and finally moves into closings. Identifying sequences, the transitions between them and the negotiation of sequences can be crucial to understanding broader issues such as identity, power and ideology.

Repair organization involves tracking when participants use self- and other-initiated repair (Sacks, Schegloff and Jefferson, 1974) throughout the interaction. This can shed interesting light on power dynamics and politeness, for example. Turn design is the most micro level of analysis in ten Have's typology, in which you examine each turn for how it is designed (and also consider alternative ways that it could have been designed). If possible, you may even ask a colleague to focus on one aspect (e.g. taking turns) while you focus on repairs, to see if you come to similar conclusions (cf. Gee 2014 on 'convergence' as a form of reliability in discourse analysis).

Another approach might be to focus on syntax in the first round of reading and then move to semantics, phonology, lexicon and morphology. By focusing intensely on linguistic systems you can begin to recognize the 'how' just as much as the 'what'. Another option might be to start even more granular than this, by looking at nouns and then verbs and then adjectives. Each layer of analysis can provide more depth to your understanding of the interaction, context and interlocutors.

A number of tools that connect with theories about discourse and real-life language use are provided in Gee (2011). These include the Doing and Not Just Saying Tool, which moves the analyst towards discourse analysis and away from pure content analysis and the Why This Way and Not That Way Tool, which challenges the analyst to consider other possible ways that participants could express themselves as a means to highlight the specificities of particular turn design.

Critical discourse analysis (Fairclough, 2015) is another approach that connects closely to the critical theory and transformative world views discussed in Chapter 1. Here the focus is on examining changes in power dynamics and societal inequalities through your analysis and interpretation.

Once you have examined the details of language use, you can begin to make arguments about how the interaction demonstrates individuals' identities and ideologies. In the Appendix (Example 1 for Chapter 10), issues of age, religion and family become evident. In addition, the turn-taking demonstrates issues of knowledge distribution, in terms of who speaks, how much, about what topics and in overlap with whom. And if one tracks receipt tokens (e.g. Right, Yes) then there are also patterns related to whose contributions are 'ratified' by others. In any transcript of naturally occurring discourse, it is possible to move from micro-level interactional details to arguments about identities and ideologies. See Gee (2014) for more on identities, ideologies and other aspects of individuals and communities that can be gleaned through the details of interaction.

ACTIVITY 10.4

Select one of the four approaches to discourse analysis listed above and use it on example two in the Appendix (e.g. videos). Did you enjoy the process? Why? Why not?

Discourse Analysis in Your Classroom

Discourse analysis can also be used with written data, which is in some ways easier than spoken data. For example, perhaps for class you asked your students to create tweets on a particular topic, or six-word stories (http://www.sixwordstories.net/) about something that happened recently and then analyse that material for particular patterns in their responses. You can also use discourse analysis on authentic written materials or on textbooks, in order to highlight particular patterns for your students. You can also teach basic discourse analysis methods to your students, so that they may collect data on real-life language use and authentic materials as a means to grasp descriptive language norms.

Tools for Interpretive Analysis of Qualitative Data

As you can imagine, qualitative data analysis involves a great deal of organization and therefore the use of necessary tools. You may find it useful to create your own tools for this purpose that are intuitive to your working process (e.g. hard copies printed out, Word documents, Excel spreadsheets, Google Docs, poster paper, highlighters). There are also tools you may use in class that can be repurposed for qualitative data analysis (e.g. http://popplet.com/). In addition, there are numerous tools and software programmes that are useful for especially larger datasets, which provide you with ways to organize, code and analyse your data more easily. You will also want to think about how to ensure anonymity of your participants during the data analysis phase. This may mean assigning participants numbers or letters and creating spreadsheets with that information in an easily accessible format. All of these issues, while seemingly minor, are essential to systematic and effective data analysis.

A couple useful lists of qualitative data analysis tools can be found here

http://www.content-analysis.de/software/qualitative-analysis
https://digitalresearchtools.pbworks.com/w/page/17801694/
Perform%20Qualitative%20Data%20Analysis

Three common tools and some information about each are provided here

Dedoose (web-based, free month trial, can cancel membership for extended periods while keeping data safe, low cost per month, same account can be used by multiple people, less powerful than other data analysis tools, upgraded often)

Nvivo (more powerful, accessible for novices, easy-to-use coding tools)

QDA Miner (mixed methods qualitative analysis, LinguistList: 'One of, if not the best multi-use text application' http://provalisresearch.com)

As discussed at the beginning of the chapter, it is important that the ways that you organize and analyse the data are organized, intuitive and searchable.

Interrelationships among Coding, Content Analysis and Discourse Analysis

Coding, content analysis and discourse analysis are methods that can be used to complement one another. In the Appendix for Chapter 10 (Example 2A, Example 2B and Example 2C) you can read through two interview transcripts and a picture of a cultural centre's plaque. Through a coding process, one can begin to see a pattern related to 'difficulty of Hebrew'. Discourse analysis reveals that Esther uses repetition with the negative construction 'I don't' and Mark uses repetition with the negatively valenced lexical item 'challenge'. There is also an implicit contrast through the words 'unlike' and 'except for', between Yiddish (described as 'simple') and Hebrew. Through content analysis, we see Esther's clear statement, 'I can't with the Hebrew'. In these examples, we can see how bringing all three methods together can provide us with a rich picture of our phenomenon of interest. This type of 'triangulation' (bringing various data collection and analysis findings together) will be discussed in further detail in Chapter 12.

Conclusion

Interpretive analysis of qualitative data can be an engaging process of discovery and emergence and it must also be systematic and explainable. As described earlier, it is important to ensure validity and trustworthiness in your accounts so that they are not critiqued for being too subjective. Acknowledging your own positionality early on in and throughout the analysis process will help in ensuring that your findings are believable as you build towards an argument. Qualitative data analysis is focused on richness and depth of the analytical issues we are interested in, as opposed to generalizability. Since this is naturalistic inquiry, we cannot control what happens and this means that things may come that we were not expecting. This also involves particular ethical concerns since we are representing individuals and groups in particular ways. It is also worth mentioning, as we transition to the chapter on quantitative data analysis, the relationships between qualitative data and quantitative data. For example, one might code qualitative data for quantitative data analysis (Phakiti, 2015, p. 33). Or, one might engage in the quantitative data analysis of observations or tracking. In addition, conversation analysis itself can be quantitative, looking across multiple transcripts across contexts for the use of particular linguistic tokens. It is important to keep these relationships in mind as we move to our discussion of quantitative data analysis.

Suggested Reading

http://www.slideshare.net/tilahunigatu/qualitative-data-analysis-11895136
This 64-slide online presentation provides key concepts and approaches for analysis of qualitative data.

Approaches to Analysis of Quantitative Data

Guiding Questions:

1. What kinds of quantitative data do you have?
2. Do you believe statistics when you read about them in the media? Why? Why not?
3. What are some ethical issues related to the statistical analysis of quantitative data?

Introduction

In this chapter, we will discuss possible options for analysing quantitative data as it relates to deductive research questions (cf. Brown, 1998; Chambliss and Schutt, 2016). You may remember that deductive research questions move from general theories to particular cases, whereas inductive research questions move from particular cases to general theories. We can conduct quantitative data analysis on nominal, ordinal, interval and ratio levels of measurement in data, including questionnaires and students' test scores, in order to quantify it and put it into numeric terms. These analyses will allow us to make arguments about the relationships between/among our variables of interest, through explanation, prediction, description and/or exploration.

A Review of Quantitative Data Concepts

Quantitative data is numeric, countable and measurable. In Chapter 9 we discussed various approaches to quantitative research design (including experimental and nonexperimental, control/treatment groups) and the notions of reliability and validity. In addition, we discussed variables and both parametric and non-parametric data, as well as levels of measurement (nominal, ordinal, interval and ratio). We also discussed the use of pre-tests and post-tests before and after an intervention, which we use to determine whether two groups are statistically different from one another. In quantitative data analysis, you seek to identify trends and relationships among the variables of interest.

Stages in Analysis of Quantitative Data

In the previous chapter, we discussed the process of interpretive analysis of quantitative data. Before beginning the stages below, it will be important to determine your unit of analysis (e.g. who, what). The following are the main stages in quantitative data analysis (Phakiti 2015, pp. 32–35), some of which overlap with those discussed for qualitative data analysis:

1. checking and organizing data
2. coding data (nominal, ordinal, interval, ratio)
3. entering data into a computer programme
4. screening and cleaning data
5. analysing the reliability of data
6. reducing data
7. performing inferential statistics

Unlike in analysis of qualitative data, in analysis of quantitative data the coding process is simpler since it is based on what level of measurement you are working from. It is very important that the coding be accurate, since the inferential statistical tests you can use are dependent on the types of data you have available to you.

Basic Ways to Summarize Results

Before launching into descriptive and inferential statistical analyses of your quantitative data, you can begin with simple ways to capture your results (Suskie, 2009):

1. tallies/frequency distribution
2. percentages/per cent distribution
3. aggregates (overall score, sub-scores)

Tallies/a frequency distribution involve your counting how many of something you have and presenting those results. An example might be counting how many of your students speak which L1s. Percentages/per cent distribution means that you divide the amounts in the frequency distribution by the total number of students. Here is an example of the same data presented in a frequency distribution and a percentage distribution:

Table 11.1   L1s of Student Participants

Students' L1s (frequency) for N = 12	Students' L1s (percentage) for N = 12
4 Russian	33% Russian
2 Mandarin	16.7% Mandarin
3 Japanese	25% Japanese
2 Arabic	16.7% Arabic
1 Spanish	8.3% Spanish

ACTIVITY 11.1

What are some pros and cons of sharing results as tallies/a frequency distribution vs percentages/per cent distribution? Which do you prefer? Why?

Descriptive Statistics

Descriptive statistics involves measures of frequency and measures of central tendency. These include the mean (the average of all items), the median (the middle number of all items) and the mode (the most common of all items). You can also calculate maximum and minimum values, which can be used to calculate the range. It is important to recognize that particular descriptive statistics can be used with non-parametric or parametric data. The median can be used for non-parametric data (since it involves nominal and ordinal data) and the mean can be used for parametric data (since it involves interval and ratio data). You can also calculate using measures of variation (range, interquartile range, variance and standard deviation). Range is the difference between the highest number and the lowest number. Interquartile range, variance and standard deviation are discussed in further detail at http://www.sagepub. com/sites/default/files/upm-binaries/46056_Pages_from_ Chambliss_(4e)_Chapter_8.pdf. Additional information about the ways that descriptive statistics can be run for different kinds of variables is provided here (toolkit.pellinstitute.org):

1. A meaningful mean can be calculated only from interval and ratio data.
2. Minimum and maximum values can be calculated for all levels of measurement.
3. A meaningful median can be calculated only from ordinal, interval and ratio data.
4. The mode can be calculated for all levels of measurement.

ACTIVITY 11.2

Find a published article that uses non-parametric data. Did the author(s) include descriptive statistics in their analysis? If so, which ones? In which sections of the paper did you find this specific information?

Null and Alternative Hypotheses

As discussed in Chapter 3, before beginning with inferential statistics, it is essential that you identify your null and alternative hypotheses. The null hypothesis is a hypothesis of 'no difference' between two groups under study (it is the opposite of the hypothesis you are trying to test). The alternative hypothesis is that there is a difference between the two groups. A type 1 error is the false rejection of the null hypothesis, while a type 2 error is the false acceptance of the null hypothesis. The p-value is the calculated probability that what you observe in your data is not by chance. If the p-value is less than 0.05, then this is statistically significant and a p-value that is less 0.001 is statistically highly significant (www.statsdirect.com).

Inferential Statistics

Inferential statistics, in which you infer how much your sample is representative of your population of interest, involves a host of tests and procedures. You are moving towards connecting variables based on relationships (Phakiti, 2015). An important thing to keep in mind is that the statistical assumptions embodied in your choice of parametric vs non-parametric data are also reflected in the statistics you choose to use for analysis. This means that not every inferential statistical measure can be used with every kind of data you have collected. Depending upon the test that you select, you can determine if your data has a normal distribution and you can also calculate probability, significance values and effect sizes.

There are three common approaches to inferential statistics: correlation, analysis of variance (ANOVA) and regression. They are described in detail at http://toolkit.pellinstitute.org/evaluation-guide/analyse/analyse-quantitative-data/:

- **Correlation:** This statistical calculation describes the nature of the relationship between two variables (e.g. strong and negative, statistically significant) (does NOT equal causation).

- **ANOVA:** This is used to determine whether the difference in means for two groups is statistically significant (assumed that the data is normally distributed). ← parametric ?
- **Regression:** This is an extension of correlation, which is used to determine whether one variable is a predictor of another variable.

Additional common tests might include factor analysis, T-tests (assumed that the data is normally distributed http://www.socialresearchmethods.net/kb/stat_t.php), chi-square tests and Pearson R (assumed that the data are normally distributed). The following table can help you determine which statistical tests are appropriate for your data: http://mnstats.morris.umn.edu/introstat/nonparametric/learningtools.html. For example, the chi square is used to investigate whether distributions of nominal variables differ from one another (http://math.hws.edu/javamath/ryan/ChiSquare.html). It compares the tallies of nominal responses between two or more independent groups.

How to Pick the Right Statistical Analysis Tool and Sharing Your Data

When deciding upon which tool to use, you can ask yourself five main questions:

1. Can this tool help me organize the data I have?
2. Can this tool help me analyse the data I have?
3. Is it intuitive for me?
4. Is it user-friendly?
5. Do I have to pay for it?

You can consult online resources that provide additional information about various tools, comparing and contrasting their features (http://www.amstat.org/careers/statisticalsoftware.cfm). Some common tools are R, SPSS, Stata, SAS and MINITAB. Excel (especially its pivot tables) can also be useful for particular tasks.

Once you have completed your analysis, you can share your data, using graphs and tables primarily. It is best if you organize these to include as much information about each variable (and their relationships) as possible. You may want to 'pilot' different versions of the graphs and tables with a colleague before sharing them more widely. It is also important to keep in mind that once statistical information is shared, it can be open to a wide range of interpretations attached to different purposes, so it is important that you are ethical in the ways that you present the information and include as much contextual detail as possible.

Conclusion

The analysis of quantitative data can range from simple to complex, from descriptive to inferential. It can involve few steps to many and simple tools (e.g. Word documents, Excel spreadsheets) to complex software (e.g. SPSS, Stata). The important thing is that you select the statistical tests and tools that fit the kinds of data that you have available to you and that you consult frequently with colleagues to ensure that your ways of representing the data to others are accurate and ethical.

Suggested Reading

Online Statistics Education: A Multimedia Course of Study (http://onlinestatbook.com/). Project Leader: David M. Lane, Rice University.
This open source resource includes very useful concepts, examples and exercises for students interested in further exploring the ways that statistical analysis can contribute to their research projects.

Section IV: Bringing It All Together

12 Arguments, Implications and Communities of Practice

Guiding Questions:

1. How can you move from your data to theories about your phenomena of interest?
2. What do you think are the three most interesting findings in your data analysis?
3. How would you explain your findings to your students? To your colleagues? To a friend?
4. What implications do these findings have for your classroom?
5. Do you think these findings can be generalized to other contexts? If so, how?
6. Is there something else you're still curious about, based on what you found out so far?
7. Whom do you consider to be part of your community of practice?
8. What are some strategies that you can use for sharing your work?
9. What are some strategies for remaining connected to others in your community of practice?
10. What do you see as the next steps for your research?

Introduction

This section will synthesize the material presented thus far, focusing on the ways that methods intended to capture ideologies and those intended to capture practices can be combined fruitfully in the pursuit of an argument, a discourse intended to persuade that establishes a position through rational support (Belcher, 2012, pp. 82, 87). It will focus on the ways that teachers can move from evidence and argument (Lunsford and Ruszkiewicz, 2013) to what this may mean for one's teaching and students. And lastly, this section will discuss how practitioner-researchers can become part of a community of practice.

This chapter in particular will provide approaches to creating an argument based on convincing evidence, especially considering one's eventual goals and audience. It will also relate back to the research questions, ensuring that the argument does in fact answer them. It will then move from the evidence you are putting forth to build your argument to possible implications for one's teaching. I will share some specific ways that research can inform teaching practice.

Building an Argument

In order to build an argument, you need convincing evidence that connects clearly back to your research questions. For an inductive research question your argument is a theory you have created based on the themes and patterns that emerged during your data analysis process. For a deductive research question your argument is an answer to whether your original hypothesis is correct or not. More effective arguments do not depend on solely one type of data (e.g. interviews) or on solely one type of data analysis (coding). Better arguments incorporate findings from a range of data types of analysis to build towards a statement that can convince any reader. In qualitative analysis your focus is on depth and heavy contextualization, whereas in quantitative analysis your focus is on clear numeric findings that can be understood by anyone. This means that you connect practices and behaviours to ideologies and reports of behaviour. This may also mean that you connect qualitative and quantitative data and analysis, examined through different lenses (observations, pictures, maps, tracking, interviews, videos, transcripts, test scores, age). They can all augment and complement one another.

Let's take one of our research questions from Chapter 3 as an example.

Topics of Interest: Generation 1.5 students, identity, peer review

Research Question: In what ways, if any, do generation 1.5 students display their identities during in-class peer-review sessions?

Operationalized Components: generation 1.5 students, identities, display of identities, peer, peer-review sessions

Let us say that I chose to collect data for this research question through observations and video-recordings of peer-review sessions. Through a discourse analysis of those observations and video-recording transcripts, I notice a pattern: these generation 1.5 students use adjectives and negated verbs when describing their own and others' national identities. I therefore have some evidence for an argument that states, 'Generation 1.5 students in an intermediate-level ESL class publicly display their national identities through discursive features, including adjectives and negated verbs.' My argument will be especially strong if I can provide data from both the observations and the video-recording transcripts. During the next phase of my research, I could potentially explore this issue further through interviews and/or focus groups. I could also include non-generation 1.5 students in my further analysis and data collection processes.

Synthesis and Triangulation

By identifying themes across your data, you are deciding what counts as part of a category and what does not. There are multiple ways to approach the identification of themes, some of which are listed below:

1. Identify themes across responses in one person's one data source (e.g. questionnaire).
2. Identify themes across responses in different people's one data source (e.g. questionnaires).
3. Identify themes across responses in the one person's different data sources (e.g. questionnaire, observation, reflection).
4. Identify themes across responses in different people's different data sources (e.g. questionnaire, observation, reflection).

For example, in my own research (Avineri, 2012) I focused on three different kinds of data analysis of one student, in order to contribute to a broader argument about the relationships between German and Yiddish in contemporary Yiddish classrooms. In one interview, the student described his German abilities and how German can sometimes get in the way of his using Yiddish accurately. In classroom interactions he had extensive metalinguistic commentary about German usage as well, in response to other students. And in one case his production of particular linguistic features demonstrated his lack of accuracy in Yiddish (as a result of interference with German). This focus on a particular learner, from multiple analytical perspectives, allowed me to build towards a convincing argument about the relationships between German and Yiddish.

ACTIVITY 12.1

What is one finding you can state, based on one data type? Can you connect that finding to any other data you have collected? How?

Inductive–Deductive Relationships

Perhaps you started with an inductive research question and from that go on to build a theory based on your data. This may lead you to another set of research questions, some of which may be deductive. In this way, the grounded theory you created can become the hypothesis you begin with for a deductive research process. For a discussion of analytic induction and deviant case analysis, see Bloor and Wood (2006, pp. 13–15). Alternatively, you may have begun with a deductive research question whose findings lead you to ask additional questions that would allow you to explore emergent patterns through an inductive research design. It is important to keep an open mind about the ways that your research becomes an ongoing process of inquiry.

Pedagogical Implications

You may remember that in our discussion of research questions, we also discussed the creation of implication questions, those questions you hope to answer about your own teaching practice based on the findings of your research. Once you have reached the point where your research is complete and you have solid findings and a convincing argument, then you can move to thinking about what they might mean for your teaching practice. These implications can be focused on the content/topics you teach, your teaching approach, classroom management (e.g. corrective feedback) and resources you provide to students, among other issues. Implications are open-ended and could apply to your classroom, your school and your teaching more generally. For example, your research findings may help provide materials for your lesson; additional understanding of your students' experience; or new perspectives on lesson planning, curriculum design, assessment, classroom management, or your teaching philosophy. The best research will be closely connected to your practice and inform and/or transform your teaching in multiple ways.

If we take the example discussed above, of the generation 1.5 students in an intermediate ESL class I could create a number of pedagogical implications from my findings thus far. For example, if I find that students not only display their identities but have a negative affective (emotional) association while doing so, then I might consider doing some activities with the generation 1.5 students in their own groups, with other activities being done in mixed groups. This would be a pedagogical implication focused on classroom management. If I find through further discourse analysis that the generation 1.5 students associate their national identities with family, respect and pride, then I could potentially have those students or all students create a project in which they discuss their national, familial and community identities with the entire class. This would be a pedagogical implication focused on course topics and projects. These are just a couple of examples of the ways that rigorous research that you engage in can then have a direct impact on your future teaching, allowing you to be sensitive to your students while being creative about your own pedagogical practices.

Students in my MA TESOL 'Language Analysis' course record data of real-life interactions, transcribe them, conduct discourse analysis of them and create lesson plans based on their findings. For example, based on a discourse analysis of two individuals reading a recipe and cooking, one group created a lesson plan focused on the use of deictics in cooking. Another group analysed an interaction between two strangers who were discussing the educational history of one of the interlocutors and the use of compliments in that interaction. They then created a lesson plan focused on the pragmatics of compliments with a variety of interlocutors. These provide just one of many ways that in-depth data analysis and findings can inform one's teaching practice. Building an argument is one of the last phases in the research process and it involves providing convincing evidence that can be connected with other types of evidence. One of the goals for our research is to improve our own professional practice. Another goal is to connect us with other people who have similar interests and goals, through the sharing of our data, findings and argument.

ACTIVITY 12.2

Return to one of your implications questions identified in Chapter 3. Do you have sufficient data to answer this question now? Is there anything else you would still like to know?

Sharing Your Data, Findings and Argument

When thinking about how you will share your data, you want to do your best to 'crystallize' the main takeaways, for a range of different audiences (e.g. students, colleagues, friends, family). What aspects of your data and analysis are generalizable and compelling for these various groups? It is important to keep in mind that good researchers engage in processes of *selecting and highlighting* the salient aspects of their research and that they can engage in effective audience design when they do that. When selecting examples, think through whether they are the 'best' examples or the most representative, being careful not to cherry-pick in ways that make your findings less believable. This means setting up your examples, providing the data itself and interpreting the examples for your audience (in writing, presentations). You can also share your findings in diverse ways (e.g. flowcharts, infographics). Webinars and newsletters, especially through local and national professional organizations, can be other ways to share your newfound research knowledge. You now have an opportunity to contribute to the same literatures from which you drew when you were writing up your own literature review.

ACTIVITY 12.3

How would you 'crystallize' your findings in a Tweet? Share this Tweet with a colleague. How did they react?

Community of Practice (CoP)

Communities of practice (Eckert and McConnell-Ginet, 1992; Lave and Wenger, 1991; Wenger, 2000) are groups of people who share a concern or a passion for something they do and who learn how to do it better as they interact regularly (http://wenger-trayner.com/introduction-to-communities-of-practice/). It includes the domain (the area of interest), the community (built upon relationships) and the practice (joint activities the community engages in). By cultivating all three simultaneously, the community of practice can thrive. A community of practice 'is not something we force people to create. We create an environment that is favorable for a CoP to develop' (Kinoshita Thomson and Mori, 2015, p. 277). It is important to have a range of approaches for learning about research and sharing one's research with others, throughout the research process and afterwards. As described, giving and receiving feedback can be a crucial step in building a supportive community of practice. This can help you as a practitioner-researcher to build a community of practice where mentoring of various types occurs and in which different types of knowledge and expertise are valued.

Building Environments that Foster Communities of Practice

You may naturally be part of a community of practice that is focused on action research (e.g. an MA TESOL methods course). As noted throughout the book, collaborative action research (Burns, 2010a; Pine, 2009) can allow you to cultivate relationships, learning, action and knowledge in transformative ways. You may also be interested in accessing online communities of practice for educators (e.g. http://www.connectededucators. org) and resources for teacher researchers (cf. Burns, 2010b). Another option might be to use a book to guide the creation of a community of practice at your school (DuFour, DuFour and Eaker, 2008).

Perhaps you are not part of a community of practice and you are interested in finding out how to create one. Below are eight steps that can help facilitate this process (https://net. educause.edu/ir/library/pdf/nli0531.pdf):

1. Connect people.
2. Provide a shared context.
3. Enable dialogue.
4. Stimulate learning.
5. Capture and diffuse existing knowledge.
6. Introduce collaborative processes.
7. Help people organize.
8. Generate new knowledge.

'Providing a shared context' could be as simple as creating a book group at your institution, with the latest research on second language acquisition. Then you can create small-scale case study research projects based on some of the topics and concepts discussed in the book and you can share your research process with the same group over time. The guide referenced above also includes six steps for creating communities of practice, along with key questions and supporting activities: inquire, design, prototype, launch, grow and sustain. Here are four guiding principles for effective communities of practice, drawn from Thomson and Mori's (2015, pp. 274–276) work in Japan:

1. Encourage learner participation in communities of practice.
2. Provide opportunities for lived experiences in communities of practice.
3. Provide variety and diversity through communities of practice.
4. Establish communities of practice to promote commitment and collective responsibilities.

In addition, as highlighted by these authors, it is important to recognize that conflict is always possible within CoPs

(Handley et al., 2006), something that should be discussed and negotiated throughout the process in order to maximize the benefits for all involved.

Multiple Communities of Practice

It is important to be part of multiple communities of practice and to grow them constantly so that you can continue engaging in research and staying motivated to share your findings with others. As mentioned previously, it is important to have the skills to share your research results with different audiences. This may be with faculty or students, at workshops, professional development days, conferences, publications and academic publications. These may be at your same school, with friends from graduate school, through local networking, through online communities (e.g. **MOOCs**), or via other means. This will provide you the opportunity to work through reflection questions and activities in this book. You can therefore also provide accountability to one another and share ideas about your ongoing research projects. Each time you share your research, you will become better at 'crystallizing' your shareable findings and remaining sensitive to audience design.

ACTIVITY 12.4

How would you 'crystallize' your findings to share them with your students, in ways that may be different from how you described your findings to your colleagues?

ACTIVITY 12.5

What are two easy ways that you can integrate into a local and/or online community of practice?

The Writing Process Revisited

The 'qualitative research text is a distinct form of cultural representation, a genre in its own right' (see van Maanen 1988, 1995a, 1995b) (Denzin 1997, p. 32). Throughout the writing process you are balancing both reflexivity and objectivity (Bailey, 2007, p. 191). We also make choices about how to include participants' voices (Bailey, 2007, p. 192), as we are then representing their voices within our own texts and for our own purposes. This is an important issue to consider when writing up your research materials. The entire process of writing up your research is beyond the scope of this book, but a couple useful resources are listed below.

Conclusion

Being part of a community of practice is an iterative process, in which you both consistently learn from and contribute to it. By integrating yourself into various communities of practice, you can explore the concepts, frameworks, approaches and questions that matter to you, ultimately allowing you to contribute to your own practice in fruitful ways.

Suggested Readings

Organizing Your Social Sciences Research Paper

http://libguides.usc.edu/writingguide/purpose
This comprehensive guide provides details about the various aspects of writing up social sciences research, including the abstract, literature review, methodology, results, discussion and conclusion.

Academic Writing for Graduate Students: Essential Tasks and Skills

https://www.press.umich.edu/2173936/academic_writing_for_graduate_students_3rd_edition
This incredibly useful book can help you with all aspects of writing up your research and includes essential approaches, activities and resources.

Appendix

Chapter 7

Example of a Positionality Statement (From Avineri, 2012, pp. 51–54)

In order to situate this research more fully, it is essential that I reflect upon my own positionality within the contexts that are the focus of this research. I have thought in detail about the ways that my own history, choices, and experiences have shaped my interest in and approach to this topic. First of all, I have considered whether or not I am engaged in "native" ethnography. Some of the issues related to outsider/insider status are raised by Fader (2009, pp. 17–21) as she examines "Jewish difference: epistemology and methodology" and by Zentella in her discussion of community members as researchers (Zentella, 1997). I am culturally Jewish, though not religiously oriented, and the research settings are generally Jewish in nature. However, there have been moments during which I felt like an outsider and others during which I felt like an insider.

In any Jewish setting, there are times when I feel discomfort because I have not participated in the activities within mainstream religious institutions that many of my American Jewish peers have. For example, I did not attend Hebrew school; I rarely went to synagogue as a child; and I was not involved in Jewish organizations in high school (or for the most part in college). In addition, though I was born in Israel we moved to the United States when I was two years old, and I have not returned there since. Therefore, there are certain domains of knowledge and experience that I do not share with other Jewish community members. However, for me engagement with Yiddish has provided an alternative form of involvement in the Jewish community.

In addition, over the course of my research in the multiple, over-lapping Yiddish metalinguistic communities, my identity as an outsider or an insider shifted both over time and through space. For example, there were times when I felt like an outsider at Los Angeles Yiddish Culture Club events, for Yiddish was used as the primary language of communication among native Yiddish-speaking adults and I was the youngest by decades. Also, in some cases, I was both a student in a given class and an observer. Even in some classes in which others might have seen me primarily as an observer, I was frequently also learning the language myself. For example, some students asked me language-related questions because I think they perceived me as more fluent than I was, and I did not always have the answers. Furthermore, at the beginning stages of my research, my proficiency in Yiddish was primarily receptive, and I was reluctant to speak the language and admit that I was doing research on its speakers. However, over time as I became more familiar with various community members and with the language itself, I became more relaxed in my own status as a member of the metalinguistic community.

There are personal reasons why I chose this research trajectory. My father was born in Iasi, Romania, in 1926 and spoke Yiddish among numerous other languages. I therefore heard some Yiddish words and expressions while I was growing up. He passed away in 1996, when I was seventeen years old. His use of and connection to the language shaped my interest in the language and the worlds it symbolizes. And, in many ways, this entire research endeavor grew out of my attempt to understand him and grasp his life story after he passed away.

My initial contact with the broader Los Angeles Yiddish cultural community began approximately ten years ago, while I was working on my undergraduate honors thesis. In that project, I met weekly with approximately ten Yiddish-speaking women at a Jewish senior centre, audio-recording the conversations. In addition, at the time I participated in Workmen's Circle Yiddish choirs, community Yiddish classes, and private Yiddish tutoring with the UCLA Yiddish lecturer.

The present dissertation project grew out of my reconnection with the Los Angeles Yiddish cultural community, first by attending and volunteering at community events and then getting back in touch with my former Yiddish teacher, at first to discuss an intergenerational Yiddish language partnership programme I was developing. Lastly, I participated in the pilot version of the community organization Yiddishkayt Folks-Grupe programme, the fellowship programme described above that is focused on increasing Yiddish cultural literacy in young adults. It was during this time that I decided upon my present dissertation topic. My relationships with parts of this community were thus already strong before I had decided upon this as my research trajectory. In addition, I have made connections with various other community members and organizations throughout the research process.

In addition, my own proficiency in and comfort with the Yiddish language has shifted over the course of my project. As mentioned above, I grew up hearing some Yiddish phrases and expressions because of my father's proficiency in the language. I also took private Yiddish lessons during my undergraduate years. However, I did not feel very comfortable in the language, nor did I speak it with anyone outside of the women with whom I met for my undergraduate research project. While collecting data for my dissertation, I have both participated in and observed a large number of beginning- and intermediate-level Yiddish courses. My ongoing exposure to the language in the courses I observed and my active use of the language in courses in which I was enrolled (e.g. at YIVO in summer 2010) greatly improved my language ability. It also provided me with increased confidence when talking about my research with native speakers and others in the Yiddish metalinguistic community. However, even after all of this, I do not use the language as a vernacular in any mundane interactions.

I believe that my previous relationships with individuals within my research contexts have allowed me to easily gain access to settings and participants for my research project. In addition, this means that there are interactions in these settings that I participated in before deciding upon my research topic, which pushed me to view this as a viable research project and frequently inform my analysis of other pieces of data. My role and relationships with others also changed over the course of my data collection process.

As Duranti (1994) and Mendoza-Denton (2008) discuss, interests, projects, and positioning can evolve over the course of engagement with field site and participants. Duranti (1994, p. 1) highlights the fact that "during this experience, [his] professional orientation changed in rather dramatic ways". Also, Mendoza-Denton (2008, p. 48) writes that "no ethnographer is a blank notepad, just as no linguist is a tape recorder" and highlights that background, social class, and subjective and affective reactions to those around her can affect her "ethnographic interpretation". Over the course of the study, my relationships with the participants have shifted over time. In addition, I have discovered that my understandings of my own history (and present) have deepened through being exposed to members of these ever-evolving communities.

Chapter 8

APPENDIX (From Avineri, 2012, pp. 99–100)

Lauren (LAU, instructor), Brett (BRE, student), Abbey (ABB, student), Unidentified student 1 (UN1, student), Unidentified student 2 (UN2, student), Unidentified student 3 (UN3, student) [Pseudonyms]

```
01 ABB: Question.
02 LAU: Yoh.
03 ABB: How would you say cousin.
04      (0.3)
05 LAU: Good question? ((reaches out right arm and
06      points at student, smiles, brings right hand
07      down))
08 ALL: ((Laughter))
09 LAU: We left that one out.  [Cousin.] ((swings
10      right arm)) Okay.
11 BRE:                        [Kuzine.]
12 LAU: Yeah that's one easy way I like that one.
13      ((points to student with left hand))
14 ALL: ((Laughter))
```

```
15 LAU: Uh [di di ] kuzine=
16 UN1:    [kuzina]
17 UN2: °kuzin.
18 LAU: =or kuzin. (0.1) Der kuzin di kuzine. (.)
19      ~But, there's another way,~ ((scrunches
20      face)) (.) which is in ((brings left hand
21      down)) standard Yiddish which I hapt- I
22      happen to (.) dislike ((shakes head)) very
23      much.
24 ABB: Hmh.
25      (0.3) ((LAU takes eraser with left hand,
26      erases something on board))
27 LAU: But it's there.
28 BRE: Can you write up ku-zin-ehh [or kuzin?]
29 LAU:              [Yoh. Yoh ] [yoh yoh. ]
30      ((brings hand up to write on board))
31 UN3:                          [Can you spell it. ]
```

Chapter 10

Example 1: "Like my parents for example" (From Avineri, 2012, pp. 199–201)

Feivel (FEI, "expert"), David (DAV, "expert"), Lindsay (LIN, participant), Adam (ADA, organization founder), Michelle (MIC, participant), Hilary (HIL, participant), Jacob (JAC, participant), Murray (MUR, observer)

```
01 FEI: Now we've been talking about ((moves right
02      hand in circle close to D)) (1.5) Yiddish
03      culture as a ((puts hands together into a
04      circle)) single whole. (2.2) Eighty years ago
05      (0.2) I don't know why I'm fixated on
06      eighty these days huh Eighty years ago [uh:
07 DAV: [( ) tsvansik]
07      [    twenty ]
08 FEI: The first- the first question would be: even
09      with among two newly introduced Yiddish
```

```
10      speakers (0.5) would be (0.2) what are you a
11      Galitsianer or a Litvak?
12      [(1.5) ]
13 DAV: [((nods))]
14 FEI: Someone whose roots are in Galicia or in
15      Lithuania,
16      (0.5)
17 FEI: A:nd (0.4) a hundred years ago the idea of
18      intermarriage (0.5) between these two was
19      ~even though it happened~ was still cause
20      for some (.) whispering around the chuppah.
21      (2.0)
22 DAV: Like my parents for example.
23 FEI: Yes.=
24 DAV: =By the way ((raises right pointer finger
25      towards FEI)) the- the- the Galitsianer
26      Litvak thing in many ways was saying do
27      you come from Austria-Hungary or do you
28      come from Russia.=
29 FEI: =Right. Well.
30 LIN: It was [also ] a labor practice designed to
31      divide Jewish=
32 FEI: [Right.]
33      =workers. So it was not exactly something
34      that was organic.
35 DAV: [Right.]
36 FEI: [Right.]
37 LIN: It was partially sort of constructed.
38 FEI: Uh::m
39 ADA: Well maybe it wasn't something
40 MIC: °You're so awesome.°
41 HIL: She knows everything?
42 MIC: She's so awesome. ((left hand points at LIN,
43      looks at ADA))
44 ADA: It didn't have to be a labor practice that
45      was designed to divide workers. [It ] could
46      be something that was in the [culture]=
47 LIN: [Right.] [organic]
48      =that the:n they picked upon. labor
```

```
49        contractors used to
50 ADA: I don't think they that-
51 LIN: They didn't invent [it. ]
52 DAV:                    [They] didn't invent it.
53 ADA: They didn't invent it.
54 LIN: But they [helped perpetuate ] those kinds of
55        ethnic (   )
56 ADA: [They- they used it.]
57 JAC: Now- now what do you mean by labor
58        practice? Like- like
59 LIN: The way they would recruit workers in
60        particular shops is that they would send out
61        a labor contractor and he would [ask those
62        kind of=
63 FEI:                                    [((nods))
64 LIN: =questions] um: partially because some
65        people actually
66 FEI: ((nods)) ]
67 LIN: believed that people were more inclined to
68        be better at a certain job than others based
69        on ideas of sort of social Darwinism but
70        essentially it was a way to build upon
71        natural kinship networks and develop a
72        workforce that was tied to one another.
73 FEI: A:nd and if the ethnicity or the interethnicity
74        of the workforce was the same as that uh- as
75        that of the boss (.) there might be less
76        tendency=
77 LIN: =Right.=
78 FEI: =for the work[force] to recognize that they
79        had different=
80 LIN: [( )]
81 FEI: =interests than those of the boss.
82 LIN: So the same way that they used sort of Irish
83        workers as scabs when the Italians were on
84        strike they would use Galitsianers-
85        Galitsianers as scabs when the Litvaks were
86        on strike and vice versa and sort of played
```

```
 87      them against each other like that.
 88 MUR: There was a Yiddish movie made about that.
 89      Uncle
 90      [Moses. ]
 91 LIN: [hiring moment]
 92 ADA: Uncle Moses.
 93 DAV: Yeah.
 94 FEI: Yeah.
 95 LIN: Exactly. Exactly.
 96 DAV: One of the best Yiddish films. And by the
 97      way one of the best dance (.) scenes (.) of
 98      traditional [Yiddish dance. ]
 99 MUR: [The wedding scene.]
100 LIN: I love that there's music in that thing too
101      hehehe.
102      (0.5)
103 DAV: Anyway
104 FEI: So: (  )
105 ADA: Heh vat were you saying?
106 LIN: (Sorry.)
```

Example 2A: "The biggest trouble I've had with the Yiddish has been the Hebrew words." (From Avineri, 2012, p. 92)

Esther: interviewee | Lily: interviewer

EST: No. As a matter of fact the biggest trouble I've had with the Yiddish has been the Hebrew words. You can't – you know Yiddish is phonetic so I can get along in it, I can't with the Hebrew, I don't know how to read it, I don't know how to sound it out, I don't know what it's like.

LIL: Yeah when they take the vowels out.

EST: Yeah, and the letters, we don't use half a dozens of those letters, except for Hebrew words, which we're supposed to memorize, which forget it, best of luck.

Example 2B: "It poses a little bit of the challenge at first" (From Avineri, 2012, p. 93)

Mark: interviewee

MARK: And it's a little, what's the word I'm looking for, a little – it poses a little bit of the challenge at first. And also some of the pronunciations there – the result of vowels being put together in ways that don't happen in Hebrew, and it can be a little, the word I am looking for, not fine, not disconcerted, but a little challenging or something.

Example 2C: Is Yiddish hard to learn? (From Avineri, 2012, p. 91)

Glossary

Affordances possibilities and constraints

Annotated bibliography a list of citations followed by short descriptions of the source along with an analysis of its usefulness for your research

ANOVA a method used to determine whether the difference in means for two groups is statistically significant (assuming the data is normally distributed)

Argument a discourse intended to persuade

Bias treating a person or group of people in ways that are unfair

Broad definition literature all literature that can help to shape your professional practice

Causal-comparative research similar to correlational research, but the goal is to determine cause and effect among variables

Closed (focused, axial) coding the final phases of identifying themes in your data

Cluster sampling 'natural subgroups (clusters) can be identified', 'random samples are generated for each of the clusters' (Wagner, 2015, pp. 85–86)

Coding the data analysis process of finding themes

Community of practice a group of people who engage regularly in a set of practices

Conflicts of interest decisions are made from the perspective of (and benefit of) one role but to the detriment of a relationship

Confounding/Moderator variable a variable that may have an impact on your findings, though you may not be able to predict it in advance

Content analysis analysis of data that focuses on 'what' people are saying or writing

Convenience sampling 'individuals who are readily available and who the researcher has access to' (Wagner, 2015, pp. 85–86)

Corpora small or large collections of naturally occurring spoken or written data analyzable in the form of written transcripts

Correlation statistical calculation that describes the relationship between two variables

Correlational research researcher seeks to understand the relationships among variables but does not manipulate research setting

Critical discourse analysis discourse analysis that integrates issues of power and inequality in interaction

Critical Incident a turning point in a lesson, usually because something unexpected happened

Cross-sectional research compares and contrasts different groups at the same time, which allows you to examine similar groups without having to wait for them to change

Cross-sequential research involves analyzing different groups longitudinally over time and also comparing and contrasting them

Deductive closed-ended inquiry that tests hypotheses and focuses on discrete variables

Dependent/Outcome variables those variables that are affected in some way by the manipulation of the Independent/Experimental/Predictor variables

Descriptive statistics measures of frequency and measures of central tendency

Discourse analysis analysis of data that focuses on "how" people are saying or writing

Emic insider perspective

Empirical based on systematically collected data

Ethical dilemmas situations in which the researcher is not sure what to do

Etic outsider perspective

Experiential learning learning that involves action, reflection, conceptualization, and application

Experimental research researcher manipulates research setting in some way to better understand the relationships among variables

Field notes the detailed notes taken by a researcher who is observing a group, community, or culture in in-depth ways

Focus Groups groups of people who are invited to respond to questions related to your inquiry

Ideologies belief systems

Independent/Experimental/Predictor variables those variables over which the researcher has some control

Inductive open-ended inquiry that moves from your research to theory building

Inferential statistics procedures that allow you to infer how representative your sample is of your population of interest

Informed consent the process by which research participants learn the details of the research and agree to participate in it

Interval the distance between the numbers has some meaning

Iterative process ongoing process with multiple steps

Longitudinal research involves in-depth analysis of the same group over time

Methodological toolkit the range of ways that you can engage in inquiry

MOOCs massive open online courses

Narratives storytelling

Narrow definition literature peer-reviewed journals and books

Nominal assigning numbers randomly to different groups in which the numbers themselves have no meaning

Open (initial) coding the first phases of identifying themes in your data

Operationalize providing a specific definition for the relevant terms in your inquiry

Ordinal the numbers themselves can be ordered in some way

Participant-observation a research method used in the social sciences as a way to understand a group, community, or culture in in-depth ways

Pedagogical implications the takeaways from your research that are relevant to your teaching practice (content, teaching approach, classroom management, resources)

Person-centred interviews open-ended interviews usually done more than once, designed to understand individuals' experience in-depth

Piloting trying out your data collection instruments before administering them to your actual sample

Positionality your perspectives and identities

Practices what individuals, groups, and communities do on a regular basis

Qualitative exploratory data that acknowledges the complexity in the world

Quantitative closed-ended data that focuses on discrete and measurable variables

Quasi-experimental research not practical or ethical to have a random sample, therefore there are some elements of experimental design but not all; cause and effect may be more difficult to determine, but it can be inferred

Random sampling goal of being 'truly representative' of population, 'equal chance' of being selected to be in the study (Wagner, 2015, pp. 85–86)

Ratio similar to interval but there is no natural zero

Reflection sensemaking about actions, the metacognitive work that one engages in to process an activity before, during and/or after it happens

Reflection repertoire a suite of options for reflection

Regression an extension of correlation, used to determine whether one variable is a predictor of another variable

Reliability consistency (the idea that anytime you and/or someone else would analyse your data you would get the same results)

Replicability the ability for a study to be replicated by another researcher

Research disposition an approach to professional practice that involves continuous inquiry, responsiveness, and change

Research questions the guiding questions for your inquiry

Sampling selecting whom you will give your data collection instruments to, designed to be representative of the "universe" of interest

Schema activation the phase of a lesson in which the teacher can get a sense of students' existing knowledge about a topic

Semi-structured interviews interviews that are based upon an interview guide (list of topics, some questions) but are designed to be emergent

Snowball sampling 'relies on the researcher's knowledge of the situation and the people he or she knows' (Balnaves and Caputi, 2001, p. 95)

Stratified random sample 'subgroups are selected', and samples are 'generated for each subgroup' (Wagner, 2015, pp. 85–86)

Structured interviews interviews that are based upon a set of questions such that all respondents' responses are easily comparable to others'

Survey research can involve quantitative measures, based on particular question types

Systematic sampling 'every nth person is selected' (Wagner, 2015, pp. 85–86)

Triangulate using a range of data collection methods that can inform one another

Validity the idea that you are measuring what you seek to measure

Variable measurable and observable means of capturing the phenomena of interest in your inquiry

References

All links correct as of 14 December 2016.

Allwright, D. & Bailey, K.M. (1991). *Focus on the Language Classroom: An introduction to classroom research for language teachers.* Cambridge, UK: Cambridge University Press.

Avineri, N. (2012). *Heritage language socialization practices in secular Yiddish educational contexts* (Doctoral dissertation). Retrieved from ERIC database. (ERIC Number: ED541891).

Avineri, N. & Kroskrity, P.V. (2014). "On the (Re-)Production and Representation of Endangered Language Communities: Social Boundaries and Temporal Borders", in N. Avineri & P.V. Kroskrity (eds), *Reconceptualizing Endangered Language Communities: Crossing Borders and Constructing Boundaries.* [Special Issue]. *Language & Communication*, 38: pp. 1–7.

Bailey, C. (2007). *A Guide to Qualitative Field Research.* Thousand Oaks, CA: SAGE Publications.

Bailey, K.M. (1991). "Diary Studies of Classroom Language Learning: The Doubting Game and the Believing Game". In E. Sadnoto (Ed.). *Language Acquisition and the Second/Foreign Language Classroom. Anthology Series 28.*

Bailey, K.M. (2014). "Classroom Research, Teacher Research, and Action Research in Language Teaching", in Celce-Murcia, M., Brinton, D., & Snow, M.A. (eds), *Teaching English as a Second or Foreign Language.* 4th ed. Boston, MA: Heinle Cengage Learning, pp. 601–612.

Bailey, K.M. & Nunan, D. (eds) (1996). *Voices from the Language Classroom.* Cambridge, UK: Cambridge University Press.

Balnaves, M. & Caputi, P. (2001). *Introduction to Quantitative Research Methods: An Investigative Approach.* London: SAGE Publications.

Belcher, W.L. (2012). *Writing Your Journal Article in Twelve Weeks: A Guide to Academic Publishing Success.* Thousand Oaks, CA: SAGE Publications.

Benson, P. & Reinders, H. (eds) (2011). *Beyond the Language Classroom: The Theory and Practice of Informal Language Learning and Teaching*. Basingstoke: Palgrave Macmillan.

Bernard, H.R. (2011). *Research Methods in Anthropology: Qualitative and Quantitative Approaches*. Lanham, MD: AltaMira Press.

Bernard, H.R. (2011). "Interviewing I: Unstructured and Semistructured", in *Research Methods in Anthropology: Qualitative and Quantitative Approaches*. Lanham, MD: AltaMira Press, pp. 156–186.

Bernard, H.R. (2011). "Interviewing II: Questionnaires", in *Research Methods in Anthropology: Qualitative and Quantitative Approaches*. Lanham, MD: AltaMira Press, pp. 187–222.

Bernard, H.R. (2011). "Field Notes and Database Management", in *Research Methods in Anthropology: Qualitative and Quantitative Approaches*. Lanham, MD: AltaMira Press, pp. 291–305.

Bernard, H.R. (2011). "Participant-observation", in *Research Methods in Anthropology: Qualitative and Quantitative Approaches*. Lanham, MD: AltaMira Press, pp. 256–290.

Bloor, M. & Wood, F. (2006). *Keywords in Qualitative Methods: A Vocabulary of Research Concepts*. London, UK: SAGE Publications.

Borg, S. (2009). *Teacher Cognition and Language Education: Research and Practice*. London, UK: Continuum Publishers.

Boyd, E., & Heritage, J. (2006). "Taking the patient's medical history: Questioning during comprehensive history taking", in J. Heritage & D. Maynard (eds), *Communication in medical care: Interactions between primary care physicians and patients*. Cambridge, UK: Cambridge University Press, pp. 151–184.

Briggs, C.L. (1986). "Interview techniques vis-a-vis native metacommunicative repertoires; or, on the analysis of communicative blunders", in C. Briggs (ed.), *Learning how to ask: A sociolinguistic appraisal of the role of the interview in social science research*. Cambridge, UK: Cambridge University Press, pp. 39–60.

Briggs, C.L. (2007). "Anthropology, interviewing, and communicability in contemporary society". *Current Anthropology*, 48(4): pp. 551–580.

Brown, J.D. (1988). *Understanding Research in Second Language Learning: A Teacher's Guide to Statistics and Research Design*. Cambridge, UK: Cambridge University Press.

Brown, J.D. (2004). "Research Methods for Applied Linguistics: Scope, Characteristics, and Standards", in A. Davies & C. Elder (eds), *The Handbook of Applied Linguistics*, pp. 476–500. Boston, MA: Wiley–Blackwell.

Brown, P. & Levinson, S. (1987). *Politeness: Some Universals in Language Usage*. Cambridge, UL: Cambridge University Press.

Bucholtz, M. (1999). The politics of transcription. *Journal of Pragmatics*, 32: pp. 1439–1465.

Bucholtz, Mary and John W. Du Bois. (n.d.) "Transcription in Action: Resources for the Representation of Linguistic Interaction". http://www.linguistics.ucsb.edu/projects/transcription/index.html

Burnaford, G., Fischer, J., & Hobson, D. (eds) (2001). *Teachers Doing Research: The Power of Research through Inquiry*. Mahwah, NJ: Lawrence Erlbaum Associates, Inc., Publishers

Burns, A. (2010a) Doing action research in English language teaching. New York: Routledge.

Burns, A. (2010b). "Teacher engagement in research: Published resources for teacher researchers". *Language Teaching*, 43(4): pp. 527–536.

Cameron, D. & Panovic, I. (2014). *Working with Written Discourse*. Los Angeles, ca: SAGE Publications.

Charmaz, K. (2003). "Grounded theory", in Smith, J.A. (ed.), *Qualitative Psychology: A Practical Guide to Research Methods*. London: SAGE Publications, pp. 81–110.

Charmaz, K. (2006). *Constructing Grounded Theory*. Thousand Oaks, CA: Sage Publications.

Chambliss, D.F. & Schutt, R.K. (2016). *Making Sense of the Social World: Methods of Investigation*. Thousand Oaks, CA: SAGE Publications.

Chaudron, C. (1988). *Second Language Classrooms: Research on Teaching and Learning*. Cambridge, UK: Cambridge University Press.

Choi, J. (2016). *Creating a Multivocal Self: Autoethnography as Method*. New York: Routledge Publishers.

Choi, J. (2016). "Creative Criticality in Multilingual Texts", in R.H. Jones & J.C. Richards (eds), *Creativity in Language Teaching: Perspectives from Research and Practice*. New York and London: Routledge Publishers, pp. 146–162..

Clark, I.L. (2005). Entering the conversation: Graduate thesis proposals as genre. *Profession*, 1: pp. 141–152.

Clayman, S., & Heritage, J. (2002). *The news interview: Journalists and public figures on the air.* Cambridge, UK: Cambridge University Press.

Coffey, S., & Street, B. (2008). "Narrative and identity in the 'Language Learning Project'". *The Modern Language Journal*, 92: pp. 452–464.

Cohen, D. & Crabtree, B. (July 2006). Qualitative Research Guidelines Project. http://www.qualres.org/HomeFocu-3647.html

Cook, V. (2008). *Second language learning and language teaching* (4th edition). London and New York: Routledge.

Corbin, J. M., & Strauss, J. M. (2007). *Basics of qualitative research: Techniques and procedures for developing grounded theory (3rd ed.).* Thousand Oaks, CA: Sage.

Creswell, J. (1998). *Qualitative Inquiry and Research Design: Choosing among five traditions.* Thousand Oaks, CA: SAGE Publications.

Creswell, J. (2013). *Qualitative Inquiry and Research Design: Choosing Among Five Approaches.* Thousand Oaks, CA: SAGE Publications.

Creswell, J.W. (2014). *Research Design: Qualitative, Quantitative, and Mixed Methods Approaches.* Los Angeles, CA: SAGE Publications.

Creswell, J.W. & Plano Clark, V.L. (2010). *Designing and Conducting Mixed Methods Research.* Los Angeles, CA: SAGE Publications.

Criollo, R. (2003). Teaching TESOL undergraduates to organize and write literature reviews. *The Internet TESL Journal.* Volume IX(4). http://iteslj.org/Techniques/Criollo-LitReview.html.

Crookes, G. & Schmidt, R. (1991). Motivation: Reopening the research agenda. *Language Learning*, 41: pp. 469–512.

DeCosta, P. (2015a). "Ethics and Applied Linguistics Research", in B. Paltridge & A. Phakiti (eds), *Companion to Research Methods in Applied Linguistics.* London, UK: Continuum Publishing, pp. 245–257.

DeCosta, P. (2015b). *Ethics in Applied Linguistics Research: Language Researcher Narratives.* New York: Routledge Publishers.

Denzin, N.K. (1997). *Interpretive Ethnography: Ethnographic Practices for the 21st Century.* Thousand Oaks, CA: SAGE Publications.

Dewey, J. (1933). *How We Think: A Restatement of the Relation of Reflective Thinking to the Educative Process.* Chicago, IL: Henry Regnery.

Deyhle, D.L., Hess, Jr. G.A., LeCompte, M.D. (1992). "Approaching Ethical Issues for Qualitative Researchers in Education", in M.D. LeCompte, W.L. Millroy, and J. Preissle (eds), *The Handbook of Qualitative Research in Education.* San Diego, CA: Academic Press, Inc., pp. 597–642.

Dietz, T. & Kalof, L. (2009). *Introduction to Social Statistics: The Logic of Statistical Reasoning*. Boston, MA: Wiley–Blackwell Publishers.

Differences in Quoting, Paraphrasing, and Summarizing. https://www.aquinas.edu/sites/default/files/ParaphrasingQuotingSummarizing.pdf.

Dörnyei, Z. (2005). *The Psychology of the Language Learner: Individual Differences in Second Language Acquisition*. Mahwah, NJ: Lawrence Erlbaum.

Dörnyei, Z. (2007). *Research methods in applied linguistics: Quantitative, Qualitative, and Mixed Methods*. Oxford, UK: Oxford University Press.

Duff, P.A. (2008). *Case Study Research in Applied Linguistics*. New York: Routledge Publishers.

Duff, P.A. (2013). "Case Study". *The Encyclopedia of Applied Linguistics*. Boston, MA: Wiley Publishers.

Duff, P.A. (2014). Case Study Research on Language Learning and Use. *Annual Review of Applied Linguistics*, 34: pp. 233–255.

DuFour, R., DuFour, R. & Eaker, R. (2008). *Revisiting Professional Learning Communities at Work: New Insights for Improving Schools*. Bloomington, IN: Solution Tree Press.

Duranti, A. (1994). *From grammar to politics: Linguistic anthropology in a Western Samoan village*. Berkeley, CA: University of California Press.

Duranti, A. (1997). *Linguistic Anthropology*. Cambridge, UK: Cambridge University Press.

Duranti, Alessandro. (2006). "Transcripts, Like Shadows on a Wall" *Mind, Culture and Activity*, 13(4): pp. 301–310.

Eckert, P. & McConnell-Ginet, S. (1992). Think practically and look locally: Language and gender as community-based Practice. *Annual Review of Anthropology*, 21: pp. 461–490.

Education and Linguistics Databases (2015). http://www.miis.edu/academics/library/find/articles/education.

Eliot & Associates (2005). https://assessment.trinity.duke.edu/documents/How_to_Conduct_a_Focus_Group.pdf.

Fader, A. (2009). *Mitzvah girls: Bringing up the next generation of Hasidic Jews in Brooklyn*. Princeton, NJ: Princeton University Press.

Fairclough, N. (2015). *Language and power* (3rd edition). New York: Routledge.

Farrell, T.S.C. (2007). Reflective Language Teaching: From Research to Practise. New York: Continuum Publishers.

Ferris, D.R. & Hedgcock, J. (2009). *Teaching readers of English: Students, texts, and contexts*. New York: Routledge Publishers.

Fathman, A.K., & Kessler, C. (1993). Cooperative language learning in school contexts. *Annual Review of Applied Linguistics*, 13: pp. 127–140.

Fichtman Dana, N. & Yendol-Hoppey, D. (2014). *The Reflective Educator's Guide to Classroom Research: Learning to Teach and Teaching to Learn through Practitioner Inquiry*. Thousand Oaks, CA: Corwin Publishers.

Fine, G.A. (1993). Ten Lies of Ethnography: Moral Dilemmas of Field Research. *Journal of Contemporary Ethnography*, 22: pp. 267–294.

Fowler, F.J. (2009). *Survey Research Methods* (4th edition). Thousand Oaks, CA: SAGE Publications.

Gass, S.M. & Mackey, A. (2017). *Stimulated Recall Methodology in Applied Linguistics and L2 Research*. New York: Routledge Publishers.

Gay, L.R., Mills, G.E., & Airasian, P.W. (2011). *Educational Research: Competencies for Analysis and Applications*. New York: Pearson Publishers.

Gee, J.P. (2011). *How to Do Discourse Analysis: A Toolkit*. New York: Routledge Publishers.

Gee, J.P. (2014). *An Introduction to Discourse Analysis*. New York: Routledge Publishers.

Geertz, C. (1973). *The Interpretation of Cultures: Selected Essays*. New York: Basic Books.

Genzuk, M. (2003). A synthesis of ethnographic research. Center for Multilingual, Multicultural Research Digital Papers Series. Center for Multilingual, Multicultural Research, University of Southern California. http://www-bcf.usc.edu/~genzuk/Ethnographic_Research.html.

Goodwin, C. (2007). "Environmentally Coupled Gestures", in S. Duncan, J. Cassell, & E. Levy (eds), *Gesture and the Dynamic Dimensions of Language*. Amsterdam, The Netherlands, and Philadelphia, PA: John Benjamins, pp. 195–212.

Google Scholar. (2015). scholar.google.com.

Graziano, A.M. & Raulin, M.L. (2012). *Research Methods: A Process of Inquiry*. Boston, MA: Pearson Education.

Grotjahn, R. (1987). "On the methodological basis of introspective methods", in C. Faerch & G. Kasper (eds), *Introspection in second language research*. Clevedon, UK: Multilingual Matters, pp. 54–81.

Gu, Y. (2014). To code or not to code: Dilemmas in analysing think-aloud protocols in learning strategies research. *System*, 43: pp. 74–81.

Guidelines for Critical Review of Qualitative Studies (2015). http://www.usc.edu/hsc/ebnet/res/Guidelines.pdf.

Handley, K., Sturdy, A., Fincham, R., & Clark, T. (2006). Within and beyond communities of practice: Making sense of learning through participation, identity, and practice. *Journal of Management Studies*, 43(3): pp. 642–653.

Hanson, J.L. (2008). *Reflection: A Tool in Learning to Teach for Foreign Language Student Teachers*. Unpublished doctoral dissertation. University of Iowa.

Harmer, J. (2007). *How to Teach English*. Boston, MA: Pearson Publishers.

Harris, S.R. (2014). *How to critique journal articles in the social sciences*. Thousand Oaks, CA: SAGE Publications.

Harrison, B. (2011). *Power and Society: An Introduction to the Social Sciences* (12th edition). Boston, MA: Wadsworth.

Hart, C. (1998). *Doing a literature review*. Thousand Oaks, CA: SAGE Publications.

Heath, C., Hindmarsh, J., & Luff, P. (2010). *Video in Qualitative Research: Analysing Social Interaction in Everyday Life*. Thousand Oaks, CA: SAGE Publications.

Heritage Language Journal (2015). Retrieved 7 June 2015 from www.hlj.ucla.edu.

Hesse-Biber, S.N. & Leavy, P. (2011). *The Practice of Qualitative Research* (2nd edition). Thousand Oaks, CA: SAGE Publications.

Higgins, J., Parsons, R. & Bonne, L. (eds) (2011). *Processes of Inquiry: In-service Teacher Educators Research Their Practice*. Rotterdam, The Netherlands: Sense Publishers.

Ho, D. (2012). Interviews. *The Encyclopedia of Applied Linguistics*. Oxford, UK: Blackwell Publishing.

Hollan, D. (2001). "Developments in person-centered ethnography", in C.C. Moore & H.F. Mathews (eds), *The psychology of cultural experience*. Cambridge, UK: Cambridge University Press, pp. 48–67.

Holliday, A. (2015). "Qualitative Research and Analysis", in B. Paltridge & A. Phakiti (eds), *Companion to Research Methods in Applied Linguistics*. London: Continuum Publishing, pp. 49–62.

Holt, D.D., Chips, B., & Wallace, D. (1992). *Cooperative learning in the secondary school: Maximizing language acquisition, academic achievement, and social development.* National Clearinghouse for Bilingual Education.

How to Prepare an Annotated Bibliography: The Annotated Bibliography (2015). http://guides.library.cornell.edu/annotated bibliography.

Husu, J., Toom, A. & Patrikainen, S. (2008). Guided reflection as a means to demonstrate and develop student teachers' reflective competencies. *Reflective Practice: International and Multidisciplinary Perspectives,* 9(1): pp. 37–51.

Hyland, K. (2010). "Researching Writing", in B. Paltridge & A. Phakiti (eds), *Companion to Research Methods in Applied Linguistics.* London, UK: Continuum Publishing, pp. 191–204.

Islam, N. (2008). *An introduction to research methods.* Dhaka: Mullick & Brothers.

Israel, M. & Hay, I. (2006). *Research ethics for social scientists: Between ethical conduct and regulatory compliance.* Thousand Oaks, CA: SAGE Publications.

Ivankova, N.V. & Greer, J.L. (2015). "Mixed Methods Research and Analysis", in B. Paltridge & A. Phakiti (eds) pp. 63–82, *Research Methods in Applied Linguistics: A Practical Resource.* London: Bloomsbury Academic.

Jacques, S.R. (2001). "Preferences for instructional activities and motivation: A comparison of student and teacher perspectives", in Z. Dörnyei and R. Schmidt (eds), *Motivation and second language acquisition.* Honolulu, HI: University of Hawaii Press, pp. 185–211.

James, C.L. (2010). "Do language proficiency tests scores differ by gender?" *TESOL Quarterly,* 44(2): pp. 387–398.

Janesick, V. (2004). *"Stretching" Exercises for Qualitative Researchers.* Thousand Oaks, CA: SAGE Publications.

Jansen, G. & Peshkin, A. (1992). "Subjectivity in Qualitative Research", in LeCompte, M.D., Millroy, W.L., & Preissle, J. (eds), *The Handbook of Qualitative Research in Education.* San Diego, CA: Academic Press, Inc., pp. 681–726.

Johnson, K. (2011). "An Introduction to Effective Survey Design and Administration". http://studentaffairs.psu.edu/assessment/pdf/Kurt JohnsonPresentationFA11.pdf

Jordan, A.E. & Meara, N.M. (April 1990). Ethics and the professional practice of psychologists: The role of virtues and principles. *Professional Psychology: Research and Practice*, 21(2): pp. 107–114.

Kaplan-Weinger, J. & Ullman, C. (2015). *Methods for the Ethnography of Communication: Language in Use in Schools and Communities.* New York and London: Routledge Publishers.

Kimmel, A.J. (1988). *Ethics and values in applied social research.* Newbury Park, CA: SAGE Publications.

Kincheloe, J. L. (2008). *Critical pedagogy.* New York: Peter Lang.

Koven, M. (2014). Interviewing: Practice, Ideology, Genre, and Intertexuality. *Annual Review of Anthropology*, 43: pp. 499–520.

Kruger, R.A. & Casey, M.A. (2008). *Focus Groups: A Practical Guide to Applied Research.* SAGE Publications.

Lado, R. (1957). *Linguistics across cultures: Applied linguistics for language teachers.* Ann Arbor, MI: University of Michigan Press.

Lave, J. & Wenger, E. (1991). *Situated learning: Legitimate peripheral participation.* Cambridge, UK: Cambridge University Press.

LeCompte, M.G. & Schensul, J.J. (2010). *Designing and Conducting Ethnographic Research: An Introduction.* Walnut Creek, CA AltaMira Press.

Levy, R.I. & Hollan, D. (1998). "Person-centered interviewing and observation in anthropology", in H.R. Bernard (ed.), *Handbook of methods in cultural anthropology*, pp. 333–364. Walnut Creek, CA: AltaMira Press.

Liang, X., Mohan, B.A., & Early, M. (Spring 1998). Issues of cooperative learning in ESL classes: A literature review. *TESL Canada Journal/La Revue TESL Du Canada*, 15(2): pp. 13–23.

Long, M. (1982). "Native speaker/non-native speaker conversation in the second language classroom", in M. Long & C. Richards (eds), *Methodology in TESOL: A Book of Readings.* New York: Newbury House, pp. 339–354.

Long, M., & Porter, P.A. (1985). Group work, interlanguage talk and second language acquisition. *TESOL Quarterly*, 19: pp. 207–228.

Lunsford, A.A. & Ruszkiewicz, J.J. (2013). *Everything's An Argument.* Boston, MA: Bedford/St. Martin's.

Machi, L.A. & McEvoy, B.T. (2012). *The literature review: Six steps to success.* Thousand Oaks, CA: SAGE Publications.

Magrath, D. (August 2016). "Interference patterns: Applying linguistic theory to lesson production", *TESOL English Language Bulletin*. http://exclusive.multibriefs.com/content/interference-patterns-applying-linguistic-theory-to-lesson-production/education.

Martinez, D.C. (2016). "This ain't the projects": A researcher's reflections on the local appropriateness of our research tools. *Anthropology and Education Quarterly*, 47(1): pp. 55–73.

McCarthy, M. (1991). *Discourse Analysis for Language Teachers*. Cambridge, UK: Cambridge University Press.

McDonough, J. & McDonough, S. (2014). *Research Methods for English Language Teachers*. Abingdon: Routledge Publishers.

McGroarty, M. (1993). "Cooperative learning and second language acquisition", in D.D. Holt (ed.), *Cooperative learning: A response to linguistic and cultural diversity*. McHenry, IL: Center for Applied Linguistics and Delta systems, pp. 19–46.

McNiff, J. & Whitehead, J. (2006). *All You Need to Know about Action Research*. London: SAGE Publications.

Mendoza-Denton, N. (2008). *Homegirls: Language and Cultural Practice Among Latina Youth Gangs*. Malden, MA: Blackwell.

Merriam, S. (2009). *Qualitative research: A guide to design and implementation*. San Francisco, CA: Jossey-Bass.

Mertens, D.M. (2010). *Research and evaluation in education and psychology: Integrating diversity with quantitative, qualitative, and mixed methods* (3rd edition). Thousand Oaks, CA: SAGE Publications.

Mills, J. & Birks, M. (eds) (2014). *Qualitative Methodology: A Practical Guide*. Los Angeles, CA: SAGE Publications.

Murphy, J.M. (2014). "Reflective Teaching: Principles and Practices", in Celce-Murcia, M., Brinton, D., & Snow, M.A. (eds), *Teaching English as a Second or Foreign Language*. 4th ed. Boston, MA: Heinle Cengage Learning, pp. 613–629.

National Heritage Language Resource Center (2015). Retrieved 7 June 2015 from www.nhlrc.ucla.edu.

Noels, K.A., Clement, R., & Pelletier, L.G. (1999). Perceptions of teachers' communicative style and students' intrinsic and extrinsic motivation. *The Modern Language Journal*, 83(i): pp. 23–34.

Nunan, D. (1992). *Research Methods in Language Learning*. Cambridge, UK: Cambridge University Press.

Nunan, D. & Bailey, K.M. (2009). *Exploring second language classroom research: A comprehensive guide*. Boston, MA: Heinle Cengage Learning. http://www.culi.chula.ac.th/Research/e-Journal/bod/David%20Nunan.pdf.

Nunan, D. & Choi, J. (eds) (2010). *Language and Culture: Reflective Narratives and the Emergence of Identity*. New York, NY: Routledge Publishers.

Ochs, E. (1979). "Transcription as Theory", in E. Ochs & B. Schieffelin (eds), *Developmental pragmatics*. New York, NY: Academic Press, pp. 43–72.

Ochs, E. & Schieffelin, B.B. (1984). "Language acquisition and socialization: Three developmental stories and their implications", in R.A. Shweder & R.A. LeVine (eds), *Culture theory: Essays on mind, self, and emotion*. Cambridge, UK: Cambridge University Press, pp. 276–320.

O'Grady, C.R. (ed.) (2000). *Integrating Service-Learning and Multicultural Education in Colleges and Universities*. Mahwah, NJ: Lawrence Erlbaum Associates, Inc.

O'Leary, M. (2014). *Classroom Observation: A Guide to the Effective Observation of Teaching and Learning*. New York, NY: Routledge Publishers.

Patton, M.Q. (1990). *Qualitative evaluation and research methods*. Thousand Oaks, CA: SAGE Publications.

Patton, M.Q. (2002). *Qualitative research & evaluation methods*. (3rd edition). Thousand Oaks, CA: SAGE Publications.

Paltridge, B. & Phakiti, A. (2015). "Developing a Research Project:, in Paltridge, B. & Phakiti, A. (eds), *Research Methods in Applied Linguistics: A Practical Resource*. Bloomsbury Publishing, pp. 259–278.

Pavlenko, A. (2007). Autobiographic narratives as data in applied linguistics. *Applied Linguistics*, 28(2): pp. 163–188.

Phakiti, A. (2015). "Quantitative Research and Analysis", in Paltridge, B. & Phakiti, A. (eds), *Research Methods in Applied Linguistics: A Practical Resource*. New York, NY: Bloomsbury Publishing, pp. 27–48.

Philips, S.U. (2013). Methods in anthropological discourse analysis: The comparison of units of interaction. *Journal of Linguistic Anthropology*, 23(1): pp. 82–95.

Pine, G.J. (2009). *Teacher Action Research: Building Knowledge Democracies*. Los Angeles, CA: SAGE Publishing.

Plonsky, L. (2016). *Advanced Quantitative Methods in Second Language Research*. New York: Routledge Publishers.

Professional Development Opportunities. http://www.tc.columbia.edu/arts-and-humanities/applied-linguistics-tesol/resources/professional-development-opportunities/.

Pulgram, E. (ed.) (1954). *Applied linguistics in language teaching*. Washington, DC: Georgetown University Press.

Punch, K.F. (2005). *Introduction to social research: Quantitative and qualitative approaches*. (2nd edition). Thousand Oaks, CA: SAGE Publications.

Rabbi, M.T.A. & Kabir, M.M.N. (2014). "Literature review in applied linguistics: A conceptual framework", in T. Karunakaran (ed.), *English Language Teaching in the Twenty-First Century: Issues and Challenges*. Colombo, Sri Lanka: Kumaran Book House, pp. 138–158.

Reichardt, C. & Cook, T. (1979). "Beyond qualitative versus quantitative methods:, in T. Cook & C. Reichardt (eds), *Qualitative and quantitative methods in education research*. Beverly Hills, CA: SAGE Publications, pp. 7–32.

Richards, J.C. (1998). *Teaching in Action: Case Studies from Second Language Classrooms*. Alexandria, VA: TESOL.

Richards, K. (2009). "Interviews", in J. Heigham & R.A. Croker (eds), *Qualitative Research in Applied Linguistics*. Palgrave Macmillan, pp. 182–199.

Rose, H. (2015). "Researching Language Learner Strategies", in Paltridge, B. & Phakiti, A. (eds), *Research Methods in Applied Linguistics: A Practical Resource*. New York, NY: Bloomsbury Publishing, pp. 421–438.

Rossman, G.B. & Rallis, S.F. (2003). *Learning in the Field: An Introduction to Qualitative Research* (2nd edition). Thousand Oaks, CA: SAGE Publications.

Rudestam, K.E. & Newton, R.R. (2014). Surviving your dissertation: A comprehensive guide to content and process. Los Angeles, CA: SAGE Publications.

Sacks, H., Schegloff, E.A., & Jefferson, G. (1974). A simplest systematics for the organization of turn-taking for conversation. *Language*, 50: pp. 696–735.

Saldana, J. (2009). *The Coding Manual for Qualitative Researchers*. Los Angeles, CA: SAGE Publications.

Saldana, J. (2015). *Thinking Qualitatively: Methods of Mind.* Los Angeles, CA: SAGE Publications.

Schachter, J. & Gass, S.M. (1994). *Second Language Classroom Research: Issues and Opportunities.* Mahwah, NJ: Lawrence Erlbaum Associates.

Schegloff, E. (2007). *Sequence Organization in Interaction.* Cambridge: Cambridge University Press, pp. 265–269.

Schieffelin, B.B. & Ochs, E. (1986). Language socialization. *Annual Review of Anthropology, 15,* 163–191.

Schön, D.A. (1984). *The Reflective Practitioner: How Professionals Think in Action.* New York, NY: Basic Books.

Schön, D.A. (1987). *Educating the Reflective Practitioner.* San Francisco, CA: Jossey-Bass Inc., Publishers.

Schuh, J.H. & Associates (2008). *Assessment Methods for Student Affairs.* San Francisco, CA: Jossey-Bass Inc., Publishers.

Schwandt, T.A. (2007). *Dictionary of Qualitative Inquiry* (3rd edition). Thousand Oaks, CA: SAGE Publications.

Scollon, R. & Scollon, S.W. (2003). Discourses in Place: *Language in the Material World.* New York: Routledge Publishers.

Seidel, J.V. (1998). Qualitative Data Analysis, www.qualisresearch.com (originally published as Qualitative Data Analysis, in The Ethnograph v5.0: A Users Guide, Appendix E). Colorado Springs, CO: Quali Research.

Seliger, H.W., & Shohamy, E. (1990). Second Language Research Methods. Oxford, UK: Oxford University Press.

Seliger, H.W. & Long, M.H. (eds) (1983). *Classroom Oriented Research in Second Language Acquisition.* Rowley, MA: Newbury House Publishers.

Selivan, L. (2016). *Seventh International ETAI Conference Program Book.* Ashkelon, Israel, 4–6 July 2016.

Service-Learning, Duke University (n.d). *The DEAL Model for Critical Reflection – Describe, Examine, and Articulate Learning.* http://servicelearning.duke.edu/uploads/media_items/deal-reflection-questions.original.pdf.

Shaw, P.A. (1996). "Voices for improved learning: The ethnographer as co-agent of pedagogic change", in Bailey, K.M. & Nunan, D. (eds), *Voices from the Language Classroom: Qualitative Research in Second Language Education.* New York: Cambridge University Press, pp. 318–337.

Sieber, J.E. (1998). "Planning Ethically Responsible Research", in L. Bickman & D.J. Rog (eds), *Handbook of applied social research methods.* Thousand Oaks, CA: SAGE Publications, pp. 127–156.

Spradley, J. (1980). *Participant-observation*. Belmont, CA: Wadsworth.

Stake, R. (2010). *Qualitative Research: Studying How Things Work*. New York: The Guilford Press.

Stevenson, M. (2015). "Researching Reading", in Paltridge, B. & Phakiti, A. (eds), *Research Methods in Applied Linguistics: A Practical Resource*. New York, NY: Bloomsbury Publishing, pp. 315–334.

Strauss, A. & Corbin, J. (1990). *Basics of qualitative research: Grounded theory procedures and techniques*. Newbury Park, CA: SAGE Publications.

Suskie, L. (2009). *Assessing Student Learning: A Common Sense Guide*. San Francisco, CA: Jossey-Bass Inc., Publishers.

Swales, J.M. & Feak, C.B. (2012). *Academic writing for graduate students: essential tasks and skills*. Ann Arbor, MI: University of Michigan Press.

Talmy, S. (2011). The interview as collaborative achievement: Interaction, identity, and ideology in a speech event. *Applied Linguistics*, 32(1): pp. 25–42.

Talmy, S. & Richards, K. (eds) (2011). *Qualitative Interviews in Applied Linguistics: Discursive Perspectives*, Special Issue, Applied Linguistics, 32(1).

Tarone, E.E., Gass, S.M., & Cohen, A.D. (eds) (1994). *Research Methodology in Second Language Acquisition*. Mahwah, NJ: Lawrence Erlbaum Publishers.

Ten Have, P. (2007). *Doing Conversation Analysis: A Practical Guide*. Thousand Oaks, CA: SAGE Publications.

TESL Discussion. (2015). http://iteslj.org/links/TESL/Discussion/

The International Research Foundation for English Language Education. Retrieved 7 June 2015 from www.tirfonline.org.

Kinoshita Thomson, C. & Mori, T. (2015). "Japanese Communities of Practice: Creating Opportunities for Out-of-Class Learning", in D. Nunan & J.C. Richards (eds), *Language Learning Beyond the Classroom*. New York and London: Routledge Publishers, pp. 272–281.

Tomlinson, C.A. (2014). *The Differentiated Classroom: Responding to the Needs of All Learners*. Alexandria, VA: ASCD.

Tomlinson, B. & Whitaker, C. (eds) (2013). *Blended Learning in English Language Teaching: Course Design and Implementation*. London: British Council.

Tripp, D. (2012). *Critical Incidents in Teaching: Developing Professional Judgement*. London and New York: Routledge Falmer.

Turner, J. (2014). *Using statistics in small-scale language education research: Focus on non-parametric data.* New York: Routledge Publishers.

Vaish, V. & Towndrow, P.A. (2010). "Multimodal Literacy in Language Classrooms", in N.H. Hornberger & S.L. McKay (eds), *Sociolinguistics and Language Education.* Bristol, UK: Multilingual Matters, pp. 317–349.

van Lier, L. (2004). *The Ecology and Semiotics of Language Learning: A Sociocultural Perspective.* Boston, MA, and Dordrecht: Kluwer Academic.

Van Maanen, J. (1988). *Tales of the Field.* Chicago, IL: University of Chicago Press.

Van Maanen, J. (1995a). *Representation in ethnography.* Thousand Oaks, CA: SAGE Publications.

Van Maanen, J. (1995b). "An end to innocence: The ethnography of ethnography", in J. van Maanen (eds), *Representation in ethnography.* Thousand Oaks, CA: SAGE Publications, pp. 1–35.

Ushioda, E. (2009). "A person-in-context relational view of emergent motivation, self and identity", in Z. Dörnyei & E. Ushioda (eds), *Motivation, language identity and the L2 self.* Bristol, UK: Multilingual Matters, pp. 215–228.

Wagner, E. (2015). "Survey research", in B. Paltridge and A. Phakiti (eds), *Research Methods in Applied Linguistics: A Practical Resource.* New York, NY: Bloomsbury Publishing, pp. 83–100.

Wallace, M.J. (1991). *Training Foreign Language Teachers: A Reflective Approach.* Cambridge, UK: Cambridge University Press.

Wallace, M.J. (1998). *Action Research for Language Teachers.* Cambridge, UK: Cambridge University Press.

Watson-Gegeo, K. (1988). Ethnography in ESL: Defining the essentials. *TESOL Quarterly,* 22(4): pp. 575–592.

Wenger, E. (2000). *Communities of Practice.* New York: Cambridge University Press.

Wolcott, H.F. (1992). "Posturing in Qualitative Research", in LeCompte, M.D., Millroy, W.L., & Preissle, J. (eds), *The Handbook of Qualitative Research in Education.* San Diego, CA: Academic Press, Inc., pp. 3–52.

Wolcott, H.F. (1994). Transforming Qualitative Data: Making a Study "More Ethnographic". *Journal of Contemporary Ethnography,* 19: pp. 44–72.

Wolcott, H.F. (2009). *Writing up qualitative research*. (3rd edition). Thousand Oaks, CA: SAGE Publications.

Wortham, S. & Reyes, A. (2015). *Discourse Analysis Beyond the Speech Event*. New York: Routledge Publishers.

Zeichner, K. & Liston, D. (1996). Reflective teaching: An Introduction. Mahwah, NJ: Lawrence Erlbaum.

Zentella, A.C. (1997). *Growing up bilingual*. Oxford, UK: Blackwell.

Index